A HOUSE

BUILT ON

SAND

SATAN'S ATTACK ON THE FOUNDATIONS OF
CHRISTIANITY THROUGH THE FALSE DOCTRINES
OF ROME.

With Diagrams

BY ROB ALLCOCK

ROWANVALE BOOKS
CARDIFF
2025

I0185252

Text copyright © Rob Allcock 2025
Design copyright © Iain Hill 2025
All rights reserved.

Rob Allcock has asserted his right under the Copyright, Designs and Patents Act 1988 to be identified as the author of this work.

No part of this book may be reprinted or reproduced or utilised in any form or by electronic, mechanical or any other means, now known or hereafter invented, including photocopying or recording, or in any information storage or retrieval system, without the permission in writing from the Publisher and Author.

The views expressed in this book are solely those of the author, and do not reflect the views of the publisher or any other parties involved in the production of this book. Readers should take the content of this book as simply an expression of opinion on the author's part, and not as an intention to cause offence or upset in any way whatsoever.

First published 2025
by Rowanvale Books Ltd
The Gate
Keppoch Street
Roath
Cardiff
CF24 3JW
www.rowanvalebooks.com

A CIP catalogue record for this book is available from the British Library.
ISBN: 978-1-83584-052-8
Hardback ISBN: 978-1-83584-053-5
eBook ISBN: 978-1-83584-054-2

To the One True God
Creator of Heaven and Earth
And His Human Son
Our Lord and Saviour
Jesus Christ

"Not everyone that says unto me,
'Lord, Lord,' shall enter into the kingdom
of heaven; but he that does the will of
my Father which is in heaven.

"Many will say to me in that day, 'Lord,
Lord, have we not prophesied in your name?
and in your name have cast out devils? and
in your name done many wonderful works?'

"And then will I profess unto them, I never knew
You: depart from me, you that work iniquity.

"Therefore, whosoever hears these sayings of mine,
and does them, I will liken him unto a wise man,
which built his house upon a rock:

"And the rain descended, and the floods came,
and the winds blew, and beat upon that house;
and it fell not: for it was founded upon a rock.

"And everyone that hears these sayings of mine,
and does them not, shall be likened unto a foolish man,
which built his house upon the sand:

"And the rain descended, and the floods came, and
the winds blew, and beat upon that house; and it fell:
and great was the fall of it."

MATTHEW 7:21–27

BIBLE VERSION

The Bible version that is used throughout this book is the King James Version (KJV).

For over 400 years, this has been the most accurate Bible in the English language, although from 1881, its dominance was increasingly lost as hundreds of different versions were introduced that have corrupted the Word of God. This corruption of the scriptures is discussed at length in Chapter XI, which details how the agents of Rome finally managed to cast doubt in the minds of many so-called "Protestant" Christians as to the authority of the KJV.

The KJV which is commonly used today is itself a revision of the AV1611 that was carried out in 1769 and is also referred to as the Blayney version. Although it corrected some spelling mistakes and punctuation errors in the original, it also introduced a few subtle changes that, to the uninformed, could serve to reinforce false doctrines. To give an example, we see in the book of Zechariah a prophetic description of Jesus, where twice he is referred to as "the Branch". In the Blayney version, the word "Branch" is written as "BRANCH" in all capital letters to imply that Jesus is in fact God. The sole purpose of this change was to suggest and reinforce the false doctrine of the Trinity, which is explored in Chapter I. When you become aware of the corrupted teachings that have entered into the Church, you can easily read over these subtle changes and have no problem gaining the correct understanding from either version; it is only when you have absorbed the wrong understanding that these differences become problematic.

I have chosen to use the 1769 KJV because, although it contains a few mistakes, as just detailed, it does have better punctuation and in the Old Testament, LORD is in all capitals when referring to God. This is very helpful as it clearly identifies Him, and in Psalms 110:1, we see the LORD God speaking to David's Lord (Jesus), something that the AV1611 doesn't make clear. When the New Testament was translated, the doctrine of the Trinity was already established, so no distinction was made between the Lord God and the Lord Jesus. For this reason, when God is being referred to in the New Testament, I have also used all capitals to highlight the separate natures of God and His Son. It should be noted that I have changed some of the words to those in common usage today; for instance, "verily" is changed to "truly" and "knoweth" becomes "knows". When I read the Bible, I always change these words automatically in my head; I feel that it is important to read God's Word clearly, in the language of the day, just as it was when written by the Prophets and Apostles, or when it was originally translated into English.

The New King James Version (NKJV) claims to do this very thing, but in reality, it makes changes that are in line with the modern versions that are all based on the Vatican-approved, corrupted line of Alexandrian manuscripts. The footnotes in the NKJV promote these fake manuscripts as being older and more reliable than the Textus Receptus (or received text) that the true KJV is based upon. The NKJV is a wolf in sheep's clothing that should not be trusted!

CONTENTS

———————

A HOUSE BUILT ON SAND

INTRODUCTION:

THE BEGINNING OF SORROWS

Along with the rest of the world, I entered 2020 with a sense of foreboding, not because of a deadly pandemic, as most people feared, but because there wasn't one! Within a few short days, it became obvious that there was something seriously wrong with the official story regarding the virus, and in the weeks that followed, I became convinced that the whole thing was a huge deception.

Draconian measures were rolled out worldwide as our governments worked together to create a false sense of fear from an invisible threat to gain total control over every aspect of our lives. Vaccines were apparently developed in record time and were rolled out under Emergency Use Authorisation, which meant that proper evaluation of the long-term effects would not take place, and the manufacturers would not be liable for any damage caused. Despite this, the mantra went out that they were "safe and effective", unless you were one of the tens – if not hundreds – of thousands who died, or the millions who were adversely affected by these experimental mRNA gene therapies that were falsely labelled as vaccines.

The fact that world leaders were willing to perpetrate this unprecedented crime upon their own people marked a turning point in Earth's history.

Many hints have been dropped that there will be another – far more deadly – pandemic, possibly an avian flu, which would also have a huge impact on food supplies, removing poultry and eggs from our diet, thereby destroying a major source of protein. It is highly likely that the Covid-19 pandemic was nothing more than the rebranding of the common cold and flu, so it isn't a stretch of the imagination that future side-effects of the Covid vaccines would be rebranded as a new pandemic! With the media being utterly controlled, there is no need for a real virus; the mere threat of one, combined with behavioural manipulation through targeted propaganda, is enough. Inaccurate mass testing with a high false-positive rate, together with any death occurring within 28 days of a positive test being recorded as "due to the virus", means that the appearance of a deadly pandemic can be created out of nothing! This model worked perfectly in 2020 and there's no reason why it won't work again.

Ever since the Second World War ended, people have speculated as to when the next one will be. I firmly believe that World War Three has already started, but that this time the enemy is our own governments, which are working together in lockstep to break down society through a controlled demolition of the lifestyle and freedoms we have come to take for granted. Their endgame is to bring about a New World Order from the havoc they are creating and then, in their minds, build back better – "Order out of chaos", as the motto of the Freemasons proudly declares!

The signatories of the American Constitution wisely foresaw the fact that a tyrannical government could pose a greater threat to "We the People" than a foreign army, which is why they created the Second Amendment. It is no coincidence that the right of the people to keep and bear arms in order to protect themselves has been under threat for several decades, as a well-armed population is far more difficult to subdue.

Just as the alleged Covid-19 pandemic appeared to be on its way out, the next crisis on the "schedule" was NATO's proxy war against Russia in Ukraine, with the media planting the threat in the public consciousness that it could escalate into a nuclear war between Russia and the West. The Ukraine conflict quickly brought about an energy crisis as the supply of Russian gas to Europe was cut off, and the cost of food, heating, mortgages, etc. increased rapidly. Russia was blamed for the destruction of its own pipelines despite all the evidence pointing to America and NATO.[1]

The consequences of all this conveniently helps the coming New World Order, as people, by necessity, will become more dependent upon the state. This dependence will come with conditions; governments will demand compliance with whatever dictates they see fit, such as keeping up to date with vaccines in order to receive the free gift of a universal basic income.

A cashless society is just around the corner, with a programmable central bank digital currency tied to a carbon credit system and digital identity. This will enable the monitoring of every purchase and every journey we make, allocating a carbon score to them – exceed your allowance and your money will not be accessible. Smart cities and 15-minute cities are concepts that are being pushed around the world as we see a concerted effort to move people away from rural areas and bring them into cities. With the population concentrated into smaller areas, control and surveillance will be simplified. We are slowly being herded into a digital prison as the masses are being fed the lie that these measures are essential to save the environment and are ignoring the dangers because their focus is fixed on convenience.

The book of Ecclesiastes states that:

"The thing that has been, it *is that* which shall be; and that which is done, *is* that which shall be done: and *there is* no new thing under the sun.

Is there *any* thing whereof it may be said, 'See, this is new'? It has been already of old time, which was before us."

(Ecclesiastes 1:9–10)

When the children of Israel dwelt in the land of Egypt during the great famine, a series of events followed that seem to mirror what we are beginning to witness today. The financial crisis caused by the trillions of dollars spent during the pandemic charade has started to take hold. Prices are increasing rapidly, with the very real threat that the US dollar may lose its place as the world's reserve currency for international trade; many nations are now looking for an alternative as trust in America has broken down.

In the midst of the so-called pandemic, a video from the World Economic Forum went viral due to its eight predictions for the world in 2030. One was that the United States would no longer be the world's leading superpower, but their first prediction attracted the most attention, which stated, "You'll own nothing, and you'll be happy." This was met with bewilderment around the world, as most people have been used to living in a time of relative plenty, where property, cars and luxury goods are the norm. Why would anyone willingly give up all their possessions? Let alone be happy about it! Something drastic would have to happen, and the book of Genesis may well bear witness to a similar "great reset" happening before:

"And when money failed in the land of Egypt and in the land of Canaan, all the Egyptians came unto Joseph and said, 'Give us bread, for why should we die in your presence? For the money fails.'

And Joseph said, 'Give your cattle, and I will give you for your cattle, if money fail.'

And they brought their cattle unto Joseph, and Joseph gave them bread *in exchange* for horses, and for the flocks, and for the cattle of the herds, and for the asses, and he fed them with bread for all their cattle for that year.

When that year was ended, they came unto him the second year and said unto him, 'We will not hide *it* from my lord, how that our money is spent; my lord also had our herds of cattle. There is not anything left in the sight of my lord but our bodies and our lands.

'Wherefore shall we die before your eyes, both we and our land? Buy us and our land for bread, and we and our land will be servants unto Pharaoh; and give us seed that we may live and not die, that the land be not desolate.'

And Joseph bought all the land of Egypt for Pharaoh; for the Egyptians sold every man his field, because the famine prevailed over them. So the land became Pharaoh's.

And as for the people, he removed them to cities, from *one* end of the borders of Egypt, even to the *other* end thereof."

(Genesis 47:15–21)

Just as the Bible predicted, knowledge has increased as we approach the time of the end. The computer age and the growth of technology has both enabled many to be deceived, but for others to gain access to – and spread evidence of – those great deceptions to wide audiences. This situation could be extremely damaging to those who only cling to power by hiding the truth from the people, which is why we are seeing unprecedented levels of censorship in every aspect of life.

Satan is the Father of Lies, and he uses deception as a weapon against us, to keep us enslaved, as he knows that the truth will set us free. The leaders of this world understand that their lives of privilege depend on the masses remaining asleep, so the growth of freedom has to be curtailed. The United Nations, the World Economic Forum and others have openly stated that their goal is to restructure society by 2030, which just happens to be exactly 2000 years since Jesus was crucified. This is allegedly being done in the name of sustainable development, to save the Earth from an imaginary climate crisis, but will be used as an excuse to justify the destruction of our freedoms.

The connection between the Luciferian agenda and the history of the United Nations is well documented and easy to uncover with the most basic of research – even its name harks back to the Tower of Babel, when the people spoke one language and were united in common purpose to rebel against God. This original World Order was halted by our Creator when He scattered the nations and confounded the language. Today, the world is once more being forcibly united by leaders who have given their power and strength unto the Beast to create a New World Order, a One World Government and One World Religion, which will honour Satan and not God.

Mass migration is occurring all over the Western World, with people, mainly of Islamic backgrounds who have had their homes destroyed by the West, being given refuge by the same countries that displaced them; America also has to contend with an invasion of its southern border by Hispanic Catholics. These mass migration policies tend to be supported by left-wing political parties, which often follow Marxist ideology, and it is these parties that benefit by gaining the votes of the new arrivals, massively changing the political landscape.

The point of all this is to destroy the nation state and break down cultural identities, making it easier to accept a One World Government, which will reflect the fractured communities that have been forced upon us. The culture clash being created by this is a powder keg waiting to explode, and all by design; when it happens, the United Nations will send in their peacekeepers, the world police force that will act on behalf of the One World Government, to restore order to the chaos that will affect us all.

Religious differences will be seen as an obstacle that must be overcome in order for peace to prevail, leading to a One

World Religion that addresses the needs of all – uniting the world for the first time since Babel.

This may well all be achieved through an "alien" deception. Movies and television have been priming us for decades to accept the probability that we are not alone in the Universe and that lifeforms far more advanced than our own may exist on other "planets". The History Channel has been continually airing episodes of its series *Ancient Aliens* since 2010, speculating that the Earth has been visited for thousands of years by these beings who shared incredibly advanced technology with our ancestors, enabling them to build the seemingly impossible structures, such as the pyramids, that still stand today. These programmes also suggest that the "Star People" probably gave rise to the formation of the major religions, as the people of the past would have seen them as gods and interpreted the things they witnessed in a spiritual manner.

When the world descends into the chaos that is being deliberately created, it would be the perfect time for the revelation that we are not alone. These beings may be revealed as our saviours, explaining how we were "seeded" on this planet by them, thousands of years before, with our progress as a species being observed ever since. Modern technology has reached a stage where such an event could easily be simulated, or it may even be real, with demonic entities posing as aliens. Either way, people have been primed and are ready to believe such a story, which would serve to unite all religions by revealing the "truth" of their joint origin!

This may sound far-fetched, but it needs to be taken in light of current events. Donald Trump announced the formation of the latest branch of the US military, the Space Force, at the end of 2019. Just over three months later, the Pentagon released three declassified videos showing encounters between Navy aircraft and unidentified flying objects.

There is one other possibility that needs to be kept in mind. Satan is the great deceiver, the Father of Lies, and it's quite possible that these attacks on our freedoms are being made obvious enough to instigate a huge uprising as the truth about the pandemic is revealed. A popular uprising could well be the desired effect; those who were deceived would join together with those who saw through the lies, united in the belief that the powers of darkness have been defeated, ushering in a New Age.

The New Age movement has been around since the 1970s and takes many of its ideas from Spiritualism, the Occult, the eastern religions of Buddhism and Hinduism, and Theosophy, the religion based on the teachings of Helena Blavatsky.

Alice A. Bailey was a prolific writer on theosophical ideas and had much in common with Blavatsky; she was also one of the first to talk about the "New Age". Bailey stated that most of her writings had been dictated to her telepathically by an entity she referred to as "the Tibetan". To quote Bailey:

"The Tibetan has asked me to make clear that when he is speaking of the Christ, he is referring to his official name as head of the Hierarchy. The Christ works for all men, irrespective of their faith; he does not belong to the Christian world any more than to the Buddhist or Mohammedan or any other faith. There is no need for any man to join the Christian Church in order to be affiliated with Christ. The requirements are to love your fellow man, lead a disciplined life, recognise the divinity in all faiths and all beings, and rule your daily life with love."[2]

The teachings of Bailey form the foundation for the beliefs of the United Nations. Her publishing house was originally called the Lucifer Publishing Company and, at one time, its New York office was located at 666 United Nations Plaza! Lucifer Publishing was changed to the Lucis Trust after its name drew unwanted attention, and it now prints and distributes material for the United Nations, together with the New Age books of Bailey and Blavatsky.

The New Age movement is still growing. Teachers such as David Icke draw huge crowds, as many people who are desperately seeking answers are taken in by these false prophets. Icke and many others expose things such as the pandemic, cashless society, etc., and this draws in truth-seekers who are already aware of such things but may still be questioning their religious beliefs. The alien agenda is also something that would be readily accepted by this movement as they already hold many of these beliefs.

Whichever way the world is going, one thing is certain: following the crowd to take the broad path, no matter how appealing it seems, will only lead to destruction. The narrow path is the right one, although it will bring with it extreme persecution, as Jesus explained:

"For whosoever will save his life, shall lose it, and whosoever will lose his life for my sake shall find it."

(Matthew 16:25)

Never before has it been more important to have discernment and be grounded in truth, as I believe we are entering

the time that Matthew's 24th chapter describes as the "beginning of sorrows". Jesus warned that we would hear of
wars and rumours of war, and that nation would rise against
nation, and kingdom against kingdom, with famines, pesti-
lences and earthquakes in various places.

What you have just read is a brief overview of the times
we now find ourselves in and how these situations may lead
to great deceptions in the years to come. This book is not fo-
cused on those things; rather, it concentrates on how God's
Word has been corrupted to leave its followers totally unprepared for what lies ahead. For nearly 2000 years, the adversary has been working against the true Church, deceiving its
followers through false doctrines so that they follow Christ
in name only. The following pages will show the background
to these false teachings, together with their true meanings.

Many of the interpretations of prophecy I put forward for
your consideration are, I believe, completely new, such as:
the two 1260-year periods spoken of in the books of Daniel
and Revelation; the 1290, 1335 and 2300 years of Daniel 8
and 12; the full story behind the Little Horn of Daniel 8; the
four horsemen; the Seven Seals; the seven Kings of Revelation; and finally, two witnesses from Scripture and history
that both point to a probable year for Christ's return. All of
these things are hidden in plain sight, but Satan, through the
teachings of the false church, has blinded us to the simple
truth that was there all along.

It is my hope that this book will prove to the reader how
the Church has been led astray by the spirit of iniquity from
its very early days, just as Paul warned about, and expose
the origin of many of the false doctrines that are followed

today. The Gospels gave numerous warnings that this would happen, but when you put your faith in the hands of a priest and let them interpret Scripture for you, instead of letting Scripture interpret itself with guidance from the Holy Spirit, it will rarely – if ever – end well!

The body of Christ is about to face its greatest challenge, and if your faith is founded on shifting sand then it may not stand when tested. The Antichrist has been amongst us for over 1500 years, hiding in plain sight, and this book will show, beyond any doubt, what was once common knowledge but has been supressed and forgotten: the identity of the Man of Sin.

The great battle between good and evil is drawing to a close:

"It is time to take unto you the whole armour of God, that you may be able to withstand in the evil day, and having done all, to stand.

Stand therefore, having your loins girt about with truth, and having on the breastplate of righteousness,

and your feet shod with the preparation of the gospel of peace;

above all, taking the shield of faith, wherewith you shall be able to quench all the fiery darts of the wicked.

And take the helmet of salvation, and the sword of the Spirit, which is the word of God."

(Ephesians 6:13–17)

1   'How America took out the Nord Stream pipeline' – Arti-
    cle by Pulitzer Prize winner, Seymour Hersh. Substack.
    com. 8th Feb 2023.
    White House press conference – President Joe Biden
    and German Chancellor Olaf Scholz. 7th Feb 2022.

2   Bailey, Alice A., *The Externalisation of the Hierarchy*,
    p.558 – Lucis Trust, 1957.

CHAPTER I

WHO IS THE CHRIST?

"Hear, O Israel: The LORD our God, the LORD is one." The words of the Shema, the centrepiece of Jewish prayer and their declaration of faith, shows precisely what the Jewish understanding is regarding the nature of God: He is "ONE!"

This point is stressed throughout the Old Testament. The Prophet Isaiah quotes God saying:

"'I am the LORD that makes all things; that stretches forth the heavens alone; that spreads abroad the earth by myself.'"

"'Remember the former things of old, for I am God, and there is none else; I am God, and there is none like Me.'"

And Nehemiah states:

"'You, even you, are LORD alone;

'You have made heaven,

'The heaven of heavens, with all their host,

'The earth, and all things that are therein,

'The seas, and all that is therein,

'And you preserve them all;

'and the host of heaven worships you.'"

When Satan was cast out of heaven after Christ defeated sin and death upon the Cross, Revelation 12:13 tells us that he persecuted the Woman which brought forth the man child. This was in reference to the Church of which Christ was head, and Satan immediately went out to undermine the foundations of the true Church by constructing his own version with corrupted doctrines. This "image" of the true Church would eventually "cause" the world to worship the Beast through false doctrines that hide the true message of Scripture, resulting in its followers building their spiritual house on a foundation of sand.

Within three short centuries, this fact about the true nature of God had been all but lost as the false church introduced the doctrine of the Trinity and enforced it upon Christendom under pain of excommunication, or worse. Around the middle of the 2nd century, Justin Martyr began to mix and confuse the simple Christian message with the teachings of Plato; around the middle of the 3rd century, Sabellius taught that Father, Son and Holy Spirit are three names for the same God. Then, in 325AD, the Council of Nicaea agreed to call Christ "God of God, very God of very God". This doctrine of the three persons in one God was fully established at the Council of Constantinople, in 381AD, and in 383AD, Emperor Theodosius threatened to punish anyone who would not believe in and worship the idol of the Trinity.[1]

Satan's plan to undermine the foundations of Christ's Church was well underway. Under Emperor Constantine, Sabbath day obligations were reintroduced, but on the first day of the week, Sunday, in honour of the Roman deity Sol

Invictus. Conveniently for Rome, Christians were already gathering on this day in remembrance of Christ's resurrection.

Paul prophesied in his letter to the Thessalonians that there would be a falling away from the faith before the Man of Sin was revealed, and less than a hundred years after Emperor Theodosius' threat, Paul's prophesy was fulfilled when the Bishop of Rome filled the power vacuum left after the Caesars had been taken out of the way.

The falling away from the true gospel, and the persecution of those who would not comply with Rome's definition of the nature of God, left the Woman – or true Church – with no alternative but to flee into the wilderness, into a place prepared by God where she would be fed and nourished for 1260 years, from the face of the serpent who sought to persecute her (Revelation 12:14). The simple truth of the gospel, as taught by the Apostles, survived, but in isolation, whilst the false church of Rome grew in power and influence as the leaven of false doctrine began to spread. Paul, in his letter to the Galatians, warned about this very thing when he stated:

"I marvel that you are so soon removed from Him that called you into the grace of Christ unto another gospel,

which is not another; but there be some that trouble you and would pervert the gospel of Christ.

But though we, or an angel from heaven, preach any other gospel unto you than that you have received, let him be accursed."

Throughout the gospels, Jesus only ever claimed to be the Son of God, never God Himself or God the Son. He stressed over and over again that he wasn't speaking his own words and that it was the Father performing the miracles through him.

The Old Testament book of Deuteronomy, in the 18th chapter, paints a very clear picture of exactly who the coming Messiah would be, and it comes from God himself:

"The LORD your God will raise up unto you a Prophet from the midst of you, of your brethren, like unto me; unto him you shall hearken;

According to all that you desired of the LORD your God in Horeb in the day of the assembly, saying, 'Let me not hear again the voice of the LORD my God, neither let me see this great fire any more, that I die not.'

And the LORD said unto me: 'They have well *spoken that* which they have spoken.

'I will raise them up a Prophet from among their brethren, like unto you, and will put my words in his mouth, and he shall speak unto them all that I shall command him.

'And it shall come to pass, *that* whosoever will not hearken unto my words which he shall speak in my name, I will require *it* of him.'"

Read these verses again and let God's words to Moses sink in. Ask yourself if there is any hint here that God was telling Moses that He would be the one who would be coming to Earth personally! Now compare what God promised in Deuteronomy 18:15–19 with the words of Jesus in the following verses of John 12:44–50:

"Jesus cried and said, 'He that believes on me, believes not on me, but on him that sent me.

'And he that sees me sees him that sent me.

'I am come a light into the world, that whosoever believes on me should not abide in darkness.

'And if any man hears my words, and believes not, I judge him not; for I came not to judge the world, but to save the world.

'He that rejects me, and receives not my words, has one that judges him: the word that I have spoken, the same shall judge him in the last day.

'For I have not spoken of myself; but the Father who sent me, he gave me a commandment, what I should say, and what I should speak.

'And I know that his commandment is life everlasting; whatsoever I speak therefore, even as the Father said unto me, so I speak.'"

Jesus was very clearly confirming that He was that Prophet who God told Moses about, as we have just read in Deuteronomy. Throughout the New Testament, Jesus constantly pointed out to His followers that they should thank God the Father for all the things that they were witnessing because it was God doing the works through Him. The following verses show how Jesus was always very clear about this:

"'I can of my own self do nothing. As I hear, I judge; and my judgment is just, because I seek not my own will, but the will of the Father which has sent me.'"

(John 5:30)

"Jesus answered them, and said, 'My doctrine is not mine, but his that sent me.

'If any man will do his will, he shall know of the doctrine, whether it be of God, or *whether* I speak of myself.

'He that speaks of himself seeks his own glory; but he that seeks his glory that sent him, the same is true, and no unrighteousness is in him.'"

(John 7:16–18)

"Jesus answered, 'Neither has this man sinned, nor his parents; but that the works of God should be made manifest in him.

'I must work the works of him that sent me, while it is day; the night comes, when no man can work.'"

(John 9: 3–4)

"'Believe you not that I am in the Father, and the Father in me? The words that I speak unto you I speak not of myself; but the Father that dwells in me, he does the works.'"

(John 14:10)

"You men of Israel, hear these words: Jesus of Nazareth, a man approved of God among you by miracles and wonders and signs, which God did by him in the midst of you, as you yourselves also know."

(Acts 2:22)

Throughout the New Testament, we see a clear distinction between Jesus and God that wouldn't even be questioned in any other situation, but the doctrine of the Trinity blinds people into accepting absolute contradictions. Jesus is only referred to in Scripture as the Son of God, never God the Son, which is a title that comes from Church tradition rather than from the Bible itself. It should be obvious that a son cannot be the same entity as his father, but Trinitarian doctrine holds that three separate persons make up the one God.

The one true God is the Father, as we see in Ephesians 4:6, which states:

"One God and Father of all, who *is* above all, and through all, and in you all."

Also, 1 Corinthians 8:6 states:

"But to us *there is but* one God, the Father, of whom *are* all things, and we in him; and one Lord Jesus Christ, by whom *are* all things, and we by him."

Jesus always gave full credit to His God and Father and taught His followers to do the same. When He was showing them how to pray, He told them to do it in secret, where the Father who sees in secret would reward them openly. The Lord's Prayer, which was taught by Jesus, is addressed to "Our Father in heaven," who, in Trinitarian doctrine, is the first person of the Trinity. Why would Jesus, the second person of the Trinity, direct us to only pray to the first person of the Trinity if they are all fully God?

The doctrine of the Trinity, as with all lies, doesn't hold up to scrutiny, which is why it remains a mystery that mere mortals can never understand. Those who question this doctrine are shamed for having the audacity to try to comprehend the incomprehensible nature of the Godhead; this situation is very convenient for the Church of Rome because most Christians just put their faith in the Church and let it dictate the meaning of God's Word for them.

The Trinity is designed to hide who God really is and control the minds of those who seek to find Him. Jesus taught us to beware of those who come to us in sheep's clothing but who inwardly are ravening wolves; this doctrine devours our ability to truly know the Father and His Son.

Paul's letter to the Ephesians begins with a greeting:

"Grace *be* to you, and peace, from God our Father and *from* the Lord Jesus Christ.

Blessed be the God and Father of our Lord Jesus Christ, who has blessed us with all spiritual blessings in heavenly *places* in Christ."

(Ephesians 1:2–3)

Paul goes on to pray:

"That the God of our Lord Jesus Christ, the Father of glory, may give unto you the spirit of wisdom and revelation in the knowledge of him, [...]

which he wrought in Christ, when he raised him from the dead and set *him* at his own right hand in the heavenly *places*."

(Ephesians 1:17, 20)

There can be no doubt that these verses are speaking of two individuals, a father and his son, with the Father being the greater in that He raised His Son from the dead and elevated Him to sit alongside His throne.

"For he received from God the Father honour and glory when there came such a voice to him from the excellent glory: 'This is my beloved Son, in whom I am well pleased.'"

(2 Peter 1:17)

In the Old Testament, God revealed the coming of his Son, the Messiah, to the Prophets with Isaiah, stating:

"Behold my servant, whom I uphold, my elect, *in whom* my soul delights; I have put my spirit upon him; he shall bring forth judgement to the Gentiles."

(Isaiah 42:1)

Are we really expected to believe that the one whom God put his Spirit upon, and in whom His soul delighted, was in fact Himself? Did the eternal Creator of heaven and earth divide himself into three separate persons and then delight in one of them?

In the book of Revelation, the final book of the Bible, we are given further confirmation that Jesus isn't God when Jesus testifies that those who overcome the world will not be blotted out of the Book of Life, but that He will confess their names before His Father and before His angels. He continues by saying:

"Him that overcomes will I make a pillar in the temple of my God, and he shall go no more out; and I will write upon him the name of my God and the name of the city of my God, *which is* New Jerusalem, which comes down out of heaven from my God. And *I will write upon him* my new name."

(Revelation 3:12)

Despite all of this clear evidence from Scripture that Jesus is not God, Trinitarians cling to a few verses that, on the surface, seem to imply that He is. The most common verses used to support the dual nature of God come from the first chapter of John's gospel:

"In the beginning was the Word, and the Word was with God, and the Word was God."

"All things were made by him; and without him was not any thing made that was made."

"And the Word was made flesh and dwelt among us."

(John 1:1, 3, 14)

The beginning of John's gospel uses the same language that we see in Genesis 1. John is describing God's great plan of salvation for mankind and, unfortunately, these verses have been translated with a Trinitarian bias, which has led to much confusion.

Verse 14, which is clearly talking of Jesus, states that He was the Word made flesh; in other words, Jesus is what the Word became. When you study the meaning in Greek of the "Word" or *logos*, you see that it actually refers to the divine reason or plan, the verbal expression of God's decrees.

When it states that the Word was with God, it isn't talking about another person keeping God company. In Job 12:13, when talking of God, he states, "With Him is Wisdom and Strength." Obviously, this is not referring to two people called Wisdom and Strength who were also with God. Today, we would just say that God is wise and strong, but reading these verses literally, without consideration to the language structure of the time, only leads to a false understanding.

The same can be said for "the Word was God". The Bible also states that "God is love", and today people might say that Muhammad Ali was boxing. These things aren't to be taken literally; they are just personifying attributes that sum up the person being talked about.

The word translated as "by" is more accurately translated as "by reason of", the grounds for or reason by which something is done. With this understanding in mind, the verses take on a completely different meaning, which makes far more sense. The true meaning goes something like this:

In the beginning was the Word, the divine plan of God for the Salvation of mankind. This plan was with God and the plan embodied everything that God stands for. All things were made with Him (Jesus) in mind; and without Him was not anything made that was made. And God's divine plan came to fruition upon the birth of Jesus, the promised Messiah had arrived in the flesh.

Contrast the above with what Trinitarians are actually saying:

In the beginning was Jesus, Jesus was with God and Jesus was God. All things were made by Jesus, and without Him was not anything made that was made. God the Father then rested on the seventh day from all the work that his Son had just done. Then Jesus, who already existed from the beginning of time, somehow entered the womb of Mary and became flesh, growing as a human child whilst still being fully God. He was coequal with the Father although He had to grow in wisdom and favour with Him; He didn't know things His Father knew and He also had to learn obedience despite being God!

I shouldn't have to point out the contradictions here as they are self-evident. The whole notion of Jesus being God falls down at every hurdle, and this chapter serves to highlight just a few of the hundreds of examples that show this.

Hebrews 9:22 tells us that without the shedding of blood there is no remission of sin; therefore, the reconciliation to God for the sins of mankind had to come by the shedding of a man's blood.

John 4:24 states that God is a Spirit, whereas in Luke 24:39, Jesus said, "Behold my hands and my feet, that it is I myself. Handle me and see, for a spirit has not flesh and bones as you see me have."

Rome would have the world believe that God was also fully man in the form of Jesus, but Numbers 23:19 states, "God is not a man, that he should lie, neither the son of man, that he should repent."

Hosea 11:9 states, "For I am God, and not man."

Apart from the fact that the Bible clearly states the difference in the natures of God and Jesus, why would we think that God Himself should be the one to make reconciliation for our sins? The story of Abraham and Isaac was a foreshadowing of the sacrifice that Christ made 2000 years later. Abraham demonstrated his absolute obedience to God by being willing to sacrifice his son, someone he loved more than his own life, as all parents would. If God was planning to come to Earth Himself to be a sacrifice, then surely it would make more sense if He had tested Abraham in the same way, by demanding that he sacrifice himself and not his son.

To illustrate this point, imagine you have an elderly man living opposite you. He is a war veteran and a widower, and he now fills his days looking after his immaculate garden and the classic car he purchased decades before with his late wife. One morning, you hear a commotion outside and go to find the old man in tears, being consoled by a neighbour. The old man's property has been vandalised, graffiti has been sprayed on his fence and his flowers have been pulled up by the roots and thrown over his car. You are deeply shocked that anyone could be so cruel. Later that day, there is a knock at your door, and the neighbour who was consoling the old man says he has something you need to see. You follow him to his house, and he shows you CCTV footage of the previous night's events that his security camera picked up. You are devastated to see that your own sons were part of the group that did this terrible thing despite all your efforts to bring them up properly and give them everything they needed. You are not only horrified for your neighbour, you also feel utterly betrayed that your children have ignored all of your instructions on moral behaviour and listened to someone else.

Now ask yourself, is justice served if you go around and apologise to the old man, replant his garden, paint his fence and wash his car whilst your children stay home and watch TV, or is justice served if *they* apologise, repair all of the damage, wash his car and mow his lawn every week for the next year? Clearly, it would make absolutely no sense for you to pay this debt yourself, but this is exactly what you are saying if you believe that Jesus is God! If He is God, as most Christians believe, then He would have to be both fully God and fully man; by definition, this would also make him coequal with the Father.

All Trinitarians will agree with the statement above, but if you do believe this then the following questions need to be considered:

- When Jesus was baptised in the Jordan, does it make any sense that God the Father in heaven would send the Holy Spirit, who is also God, to land upon Jesus, who is God, too?

  "And lo, a voice from heaven saying, 'This is my beloved Son in whom I am well pleased.'"

  (Matthew 3:17)

- How can Jesus be the Christ, the Messiah, the Anointed One of God if he is God?

  (Acts 10:38)

- How could Satan try to tempt Jesus (God) who created everything, including Himself, by offering Him all the kingdoms of Earth?

  (Luke 4:1-13)

- How was Jesus fully tempted in all ways if God can't be tempted?

  (Hebrews 4:15 & James 1:13)

- Why did the demons identify Him as the Son of God or the Holy One of God?

  (Mark 1:24 & Matthew 8:29)

- How could Jesus increase in wisdom and in favour with God if He is God?

  (Luke 2:52)

- Why did Jesus say that it would be forgiven to blaspheme against Him but not against the Holy Spirit when, in the Trinity, both are equally God?

  (Matthew 12:32)

- Why would Jesus constantly make it clear that He wasn't speaking His own words or performing His own miracles? If Jesus was fully God, then they would be His own.

  (John 14:10 & Acts 2:22)

- How can Jesus be the mediator between God and men if He is God?

  (1 Timothy 2:5)

- How is it that nobody, including Jesus, knows when the last day will be apart from the Father? If Jesus was fully God, He would know this too.

  (Mark 13:32)

- If Jesus is fully God, why would He pray to Himself in the Garden of Gethsemane saying, "O my Father, if it be possible, let this cup pass from me; nevertheless, not as I will, but as you *will*."

(Matthew 26:39)

- How did He obtain a more excellent name by inheritance than the angels? As God, He would already have the most excellent name there is.

(Hebrews 1:4)

- If Jesus was fully God, how could He die? God is immortal.

(John 19:33 & 1 Timothy 1:17)

- And if Jesus didn't really die, then where was the sacrifice?

(Hebrews 10:12)

- How can Jesus sit at the right hand of God if He is God?

(Romans 8:34)

- How could Jesus inherit the kingdom? If He is God, the kingdom was always His.

(Hebrews 2:7–8)

To believe these things, you have to put all common sense on hold and just have blind faith in an unfathomable mystery. This is precisely what Rome has always demanded, as it was the Synagogue of Satan that came up with this ridiculous and highly damaging doctrine in the first place – Rome has always tried to make everyone believe that the Bible is a mystery beyond our understanding and that we should trust in her to interpret doctrine for us.

The Trinity is the most damaging of all doctrines because it undermines the very foundation of our faith. If you say that Jesus is actually God, then there was no real sacrifice because God cannot die. Jesus the man, and all of His incredible achievements on behalf of mankind, are lost; the Trinity means that God was just playing the role of a man and that Satan's constant accusation that mankind is not worthy of God would be true.

The first Adam failed to fight temptation, transgressed God's law and brought sin and death into the world. The Second Adam, Jesus Christ, was fully tempted, as we are, yet he didn't sin and was obedient unto the Cross, defeating both sin and death on behalf of us all.

Not only does the doctrine of the Trinity destroy our understanding of the true relationship between God and His Son, but it is also the biggest stumbling block to Jews accepting that their Messiah has come. The Jewish nation has always known that God is one and that their Messiah would be a descendant of King David, in the flesh (John 7:42). Satan's masterplan ensures that the vast majority of God's chosen people will never accept their Messiah and that Christians, who do accept Him, have no idea who He actually is. By not acknowledging the separate identities and natures of Jesus and His Father, you do a terrible injustice to them both.

I urge you to think carefully about the words Jesus spoke when He was praying to His God and Father on the night before his Crucifixion:

"'And this is life eternal, that they might know you, the only true God, and Jesus Christ whom you have sent.'"

(John 17:3)

1   Stannus, Hugh H., *History of The Origin of The Doctrine of The Trinity in The Christian Church*, p.8. Christian Life Publishing Company, 281 Strand London. 1883.

CHAPTER II

WHO IS THE ANTICHRIST?

The vast majority of the Christian world has been deceived into believing that the Antichrist is an individual who will appear on the world stage towards the end of the age to fulfil the 70th week of Daniel's prophecy, by causing the sacrifice and oblation to cease in a rebuilt third temple. This doctrine was conceived and propagated around the world by forces acting on behalf of the actual Antichrist, who has been working hard to hide his true identity for over 1500 years.

Antichrist does not just mean "against Christ", as is often thought, it also means "taking the place of Christ". This is not achieved by a single evil man; rather, it is an office, like the President of the United States or the Prime Minister of Great Britain. Jesus said that many would come in His name claiming to be Christ, and this is precisely what has happened.

Just as the Bible is very clear when it comes to the identity of the Christ, it also leaves us in no doubt as to the identity of the Antichrist. The book of Daniel gives us the first clear picture that describes the origin and identity of this man. In

Daniel's second chapter, he interprets King Nebuchadnezzar's dream, describing four great kingdoms upon the Earth,
starting with Babylon, symbolised by the four different metal sections that made up the great image in the king's dream.

In the seventh chapter, Daniel has a dream that gives
more details about these four kingdoms upon the Earth. Babylon would be defeated by the Medo-Persian Empire, which
in turn would be defeated by a third empire, revealed in Daniel's eighth chapter as Greece. Greece is then defeated by a
fourth, which will be the final kingdom/empire upon Earth.

In his dream, Daniel sees all of these kingdoms as beasts:
Babylon a lion, Medo-Persia a bear and Greece a leopard,
but the fourth is unlike any known beast, being described
as dreadful and terrible and strong exceedingly, and having
ten horns. As Daniel watches, he sees another, a little horn,
coming up among the ten, before whom three of the first
horns are plucked up by the roots; this horn has eyes like
a man and a mouth speaking great things. The Little Horn
goes on to make war with the saints – and prevail against
them for a time, times and the dividing of time – until his
dominion is taken away and destroyed when the Ancient of
Days comes. Judgement is given to His Saints and the time
comes that they possess the kingdom.

The time period above is mentioned many times in Scripture, although it is represented in different ways. Forty-two
months and 1260 days are both used, but the amount of
time is the same. "A time" refers to a Biblical year, which
consists of 360 days; "times" is two years, and the dividing
of time", half a year. Added together, we get three and a half
years, forty-two months or 1260 days. In prophecy, "a day"

is counted for a year, so this time period always refers to 1260 years. (See Numbers 14:34 & Ezekiel 4:6)

The person being described by Daniel as "the Little Horn" goes by many other names: the Man of Sin, the Son of Perdition, the Earth Beast and the False Prophet, but his most well-known name is the Antichrist. Using the historical record, Daniel's description alone gives us enough information to identify this man, but many other books of the Bible, particularly 2 Thessalonians and Revelation, combine to leave us in no doubt.

Rome is the power that replaced Greece as the fourth great kingdom/empire upon the Earth, and it was indeed dreadful and terrible and strong exceedingly. As Rome grew, it separated into ten regions, symbolised by the ten horns seen in Daniel's vision. In 476AD, the Western Empire appeared to fall as the power of the Caesars ended; this was the head wound to the beast as described in Revelation 13:3.

When Paul wrote to the Thessalonians, he warned that there would be a falling away from the true faith before the Man of Sin, the Son of Perdition, would be revealed. Paul went on to say:

"For the mystery of iniquity does already work: only he who now restrains *will restrain*, until he be taken out of the way.

And then shall that Wicked be revealed, whom the Lord shall consume with the spirit of his mouth and shall destroy with the brightness of his coming."

We know from Daniel's vision that Paul's description of the Man of Sin is the same person as the Little Horn who will be destroyed at Christ's Second Coming, but we also get a second clue, which fits perfectly with the history surrounding the apparent fall of the Western Roman Empire, as previously stated. Paul's description of the one restraining in his day (the Caesars) being taken out of the way, leading to the revealing of the Man of Sin, is a perfect match for what happened in 476 AD when the Roman beast suffered its deadly head wound. However, this wound was healed when the Bishop of Rome filled the power vacuum left by the Caesars to preside over the divided nations of the Western Empire.

This new Little Horn now grew among the ten and would go on to pluck up three of them by the roots before reaching full power. Not long after the healing of the head wound to the Roman beast, we see that:

"[...] he was given a mouth speaking great things and blasphemies, and power was given unto him to continue forty-two months" (1260 years).

(Revelation 13:5)

In 607 AD, Emperor Phocas made Boniface III the last Bishop and the first Pope of Rome.[1] The Papacy is, was and always will be the Antichrist of prophecy. As we shall see, this office fulfils every last detail given in Scripture; no other power even comes close to being a contender for the Man of Sin.

Revelation 12 describes a great red dragon having seven heads and ten horns and seven crowns upon its heads. The dragon stood before the Woman, who was ready to deliver, to devour her Child as soon as it was born. And she brought forth a male Child, who was to rule all nations with a rod of iron: and her Child was caught up unto God and to His throne.

In Scripture, the Woman is symbolic of the Church, and the vision just described clearly points to the birth of Jesus in the region occupied by Rome, which was under the influence of Satan, the great red dragon. Jesus is ultimately killed by this beast kingdom and is resurrected to sit at the right hand of God's throne.

Here, Rome is diverse from all of the other beasts as it is a combination of them, having retained features of all the previous kingdoms, which is why it is seen to have seven heads. In Daniel's dream, Babylon is seen as a lion with one head; Medo-Persia a bear, the second head; Greece is described as a leopard with four heads, making six. Together with Rome, which has its own head, we arrive at seven heads in total for the Roman beast. It also has ten horns, symbolic of the ten regions that made up the Roman Empire, and seven crowns upon the heads, showing that this beast kingdom is united and has full control.

The following chapter (Revelation 13) describes a beast rising up out of the sea, having seven heads and ten horns, and upon his horns ten crowns. The beast John sees here is like a leopard, with the feet of a bear and the mouth of a lion; and the dragon gave the beast his power and his throne and great authority. This description of the beast rising up is almost identical to the one we saw in Revelation 12, the only difference being that the crowns have gone from the heads of the beast and now there are ten of them upon the horns. The description suggests not a new beast but a new phase in the life of the Revelation 12 beast, where the power is no longer united but divided.

History shows that this is another confirmation of what happened just prior to the beast receiving the deadly head wound. In 312 AD, Constantine the Great became the ruler of Rome after seeing a vision of a cross of light above the sun before winning the Battle of Milvian Bridge. The following year, he legalised Christianity throughout the empire but, although professing to Christianity, continued many Pagan practices of old, rebranding them to appear Christian. It didn't take long for this leaven to spread. Constantine convened councils to dictate doctrine to be followed throughout Christendom; it was under Constantine that the false doctrine of the Trinity was agreed upon. He also reinstituted the Sabbath and changed it from the seventh day of the week to the first (Sunday) in honour of the Roman God, Sol Invictus, causing people to again be subject to the law that Christ had fulfilled. (See Chapter X.)

This was the falling away spoken of by Paul in his letter to the Thessalonians and was a precursor to the revealing of the Man of Sin. Only 150 years after the Council of Nicaea, this newly emerging phase of the Roman fourth beast suffered a deadly head wound when the Western Roman Empire fell in 476 AD, and the crowns found themselves on the ten horns that made up the now divided empire. This would have been the end of the beast had it not been for the Bishop of Rome, who filled the power vacuum left by the Caesars. As Christianity, despite being corrupted, had spread throughout the empire, the Roman Bishop was greatly respected, and his spiritual authority and recognition was sought by the horns who would receive power as kings one hour with the beast. So, the head wound began to heal and all the world wondered after the beast.

The power offered by Satan to Jesus, to rule over all the kingdoms of Earth, was rejected, as Christ had no intention of exchanging the anointing He received in the Jordan from His Father for earthly gain. The offer rejected by Jesus was willingly accepted by the Papacy; the Pope became Satan's anointed one, the Antichrist, receiving power, his throne and great authority from the Father of Lies, the great red dragon.

As time went by, Daniel's prophecy was realised when first one horn, the Vandals, then a second, the Ostrogoths, fell to the armies fighting on behalf of the Man of Sin to remove all threats to his growth to ultimate power and authority. In 774AD, the Frankish King Charlemagne defeated the Lombards on behalf of the Pope, removing the final horn standing in the way of the Pope's rise to supremacy over not just spiritual but also temporal power. As reward for Charlemagne's loyalty and the donation of these conquered lands (first promised to the Papacy by his father Pepin), he was crowned Emperor of the Holy Roman Empire by Pope Leo III on Christmas Day, 800AD.

Then, 300 years after the third horn was uprooted, the Man of Sin finally reached the height of his power, when Hildebrand, Pope Gregory VII, ascended the Chair of St Peter and declared that as the representative of deity on Earth, the Pope was now above kings and emperors, and subject to no man.[2] With Gregory's Pontificate, a prophetic clock was started, and the 1260 years that Antichrist had been given to "continue" began, with the Pope sitting in the Temple of God, showing himself that he is God, as prophesied by Paul (Revelation 13:5 & 2 Thessalonians 2:4).

The Little Horn seen by Daniel was now speaking great things and blasphemies against the Most High, and the wearing out of the Saints was about to begin. In 1198 AD, under Pope Innocent III, the full-scale war against the Saints was enacted with the genocidal slaughter of all those who would not accept the spiritual authority of the Pope. Throughout the centuries that followed, tens of millions died, either openly, at the hands of forces working for the Papacy, or covertly, through wars (including both World Wars) that served to punish the people and countries that had not accepted the supremacy of the Pope. All of this suffering and death to satisfy the thirst of the Woman, drunk with the blood of the Saints and with the blood of the Martyrs of Jesus, as foreseen by John in Revelation 17.

The remnant of true believers, such as the Waldensians and Albigenses, who had kept to the original gospel, were nearly wiped out after having been nourished in the wilderness for 1260 years from the face of the serpent. The dragon was now angry with the Woman – or the true Church – and went to make war with the remnant of her offspring, who keep the Commandments of God and have the testimony of Jesus Christ (Revelation 12:14–17).

If any proof were needed that the Bible contains the very Word of God, one need look no further than the precise fulfilment of Daniel's prophecy in every detail as outlined above. Daniel's prophetic words were written in the 6th century before Christ, and even if you accept some scholars' date of the 2nd century BC, you still have a perfect description of events that happened over 1000 years in the future!

The beast that John sees rising out of the sea in Revelation 13 is clearly the Pagan Roman Empire as it appears to transition from Paganism to Christianity. The beast that rises out of the Earth is the Papacy, which is the Little Horn that rises out of the head of the fourth beast, following the receiving and healing of the head wound in 476AD.

The Seventh Day Adventist Church (SDA) holds to an altogether different teaching on the beasts of Revelation 13, and their version has become widely accepted despite being totally at odds with Scripture. The SDA teaches that the Papacy is the first beast (or sea beast) and America is the second beast out of the Earth.[3] Adventists teach that the Antichrist Papal power began its 1260-year reign in 538AD with the enactment of the decree of Justinian, and ended in 1798AD with the French Revolution, which they say was the deadly head wound.[4] The head wound was then healed in 1929 with the Lateran Treaty, where the Papacy regained temporal power when Vatican City became a city state, independent from Italy.

The SDA had to make the Papacy appear to be the first beast of Revelation 13 in order to make room for America to become the second beast. They point out that America becoming independent in 1776 was the rising of the Earth beast, just as the Papacy's power was coming to an end, a little over 20 years later. The description of this new beast having two horns like a lamb is said to be symbolic of the buffalo, a beast often associated with America. America is said to exercise all the power of the first beast before it (the Papacy) and cause all the world to worship this first beast by fighting on behalf of, and working to further the interests of, the Pope of Rome.

Both SDA descriptions of these beasts sound very plausible on the surface, but look a little deeper and you will find huge problems that rule them out completely. Revelation 13 is very clear when it states that the sea beast, which is seen rising up, suffers a deadly head wound that is then healed *before* it is given a mouth speaking great things and blasphemies, which we know refers to the Papacy. It is then given power to continue for forty-two months (1260 years). Daniel 7:25 foretold this event when it talks of the Little Horn speaking great words against the Most High and wearing out the Saints until a time, times and the dividing of time (1260 years). Previous to this, Daniel 7:21– 22 points out that the Little Horn (the Papacy) made war with the Saints and prevailed against them until the Ancient of Days came and judgement was given to the Saints of the Most High.

We have just seen that the head wound and healing occurred prior to the Papacy's rise, so how can it be the Papacy that suffers the head wound? Scripture tells us in many places that the Antichrist power is in control until it is destroyed by the Second Coming of Christ, as we saw above and in 2 Thessalonians 2:8, where Paul speaks of the Wicked One whom the Lord shall consume with the Spirit of His mouth and shall destroy with the brightness of His coming. It is very clear that the Pope is still in control over the kings and governments of the Earth and that his reign is far from over, so the 1260 years he is given to "continue" cannot have ended over 200 years ago, as the Adventists claim.

America being the second or Earth beast is another huge mistake. The book of Daniel, which is Revelation's twin, tells the story of Earth's history from Babylon until the Second Coming of Christ. Both chapters two and seven paint a picture of the four great kingdoms upon the Earth, and the only other power mentioned is the Little Horn – which rises out of the head of the fourth beast kingdom to become the final phase of the fourth beast, which remains in power until Christ's return. Daniel doesn't even hint at another power that could imply America, so are we to believe that he overlooked this detail that the SDA teaches? Or could it be that Daniel's vision of the fourth beast and the Little Horn power is actually a perfect match for the two beasts of Revelation 13: Pagan Rome and the Papacy!

The Pope appears lamblike (Christlike) but speaks as a dragon. He exercises all the power of the first beast before him (Pagan Rome) and causes all the Earth to worship the first beast whose deadly wound was healed. The Catholic Church "causes" the Earth to worship the first beast because Catholicism is nothing more than Paganism disguised as Christianity. The doctrines of this false church – such as infant Baptism, the Sacraments, Lent, Easter, Christmas, the Trinity and the Sunday Sabbath – have been accepted by the vast majority of the Christian world, which is why the Catholic Church is described as:

"MYSTERY, BABYLON THE GREAT, THE MOTHER OF HARLOTS AND ABOMINATIONS OF THE EARTH."
(Revelation 17:5)

The "image to the beast" is a perfect description of this false religious system because it is an image, or copy, of true Christianity. By worshipping this image, your worship is actually going to the beast, which had the wound by a sword and did live: Pagan Rome, which is the power controlled by Satan, the great red dragon.

Revelation 13:14 states that the Earth beast:

"deceives them that dwell on the earth by *the means of* those miracles which he had power to do in the sight of the beast" (referring to the first, or sea, beast).

There is a parallel verse to this in Revelation 19:20 that states:

"And the beast was taken, and with him the false prophet that worked miracles before him".

We can see from this that the Earth beast is identified as the false prophet and that he will face destruction, together with the other beast (the sea beast) when Christ returns. (See Chapter XIV.)

Scripture reveals that Christ is the true Prophet. In Deuteronomy 18:18, God says in relation to Jesus:

"I will raise them up a Prophet from among their brethren, like unto you, and will put my words in his mouth, and he shall speak unto them all that I shall command him."

If, therefore, Jesus is the Christ, the true Prophet, then doesn't it make sense that the Pope is the Antichrist, the false prophet? If the false prophet and the Earth beast are one and the same, as seen above, then this completely rules out America as the aforementioned beast from the Earth.

It is well known that the Jesuits infiltrated the SDA, but how much influence they had over this teaching may never be known.[5] By making the Papacy the first beast of Revelation 13, the spotlight was taken off the Pope and the threat he still poses – his 1260-year reign continues to this day.

With the invention of the printing press in the 15th century, the Papacy faced its greatest threat: the Bible came within reach of the common man. Prior to this, the Bible was only to be read in church – and in Latin – to keep the laity ignorant of the true gospel, which would expose the Catholic Church, the Synagogue of Satan, for who it really was.

The true Church is described in the book of Revelation as the Woman who fled into the wilderness following the stoning of Steven, when the gospel went to the Gentiles – the event that marked the end of Daniel's 70th week. These true followers of the uncorrupted gospel (as taught by the Apostles) would laboriously copy the scriptures by hand, so it was a tremendous loss when they were destroyed, together with their owners, when discovered by the Papal Inquisition.

God raised up great men to fight against this darkness by translating His Word into the common tongue. In 1517, Martin Luther directly challenged the corruption of the Church and the authority of the Pope through his 95 theses, which he famously nailed to the door of All Saints Church in Wittenberg, starting the Protestant Reformation.

To counter this challenge, Satan raised an army in the form of the Society of Jesus (better known as the Jesuits), founded by Ignatius of Loyola, who swore to destroy the Protestant Reformation by any means necessary. In 1545, the Council of Trent was convened, where the Catholic Church condemned the heresy of Protestantism and tried to reestablish its own doctrines and authority over the Christian world. Loyola and his Jesuits were given the full blessing of the Papacy to destroy the Protestants and their Bible, which was placed on the church's list of prohibited books.

Bibles were being printed faster than they could be destroyed, and as knowledge increased, the lies of the false church were beginning to be exposed. Erasmus first published his Greek New Testament, based on the received text (or Textus Receptus) in 1516, just prior to the Reformation started by Luther. The received text was from a line of manuscripts originating from Antioch, where Christianity was first named. This line, also known as the Majority Text, formed the basis for Erasmus's work, which led to the most well-known and accurate Bible in the English language: the King James Version of 1611.

When King James announced his commission for the translation of a new Bible in 1604, the Jesuits immediately plotted to destroy the work and the King of England with it – something we know today as the gunpowder plot of 1605. The story of this plot has been twisted over the years to make the Jesuits out to be the poor victims fighting against the persecution of Catholics at the hand of the English Crown. The plot failed, the plotters were executed, and the King James Bible went on to become the greatest Bible of all time, and a huge thorn in the side of the Papacy, who hated it with a passion.

The Jesuits would go on to institute a system of learning against learning, infiltrating and controlling centres of education around the world. They also controlled media and entertainment, the sciences and medicine. The Bible couldn't be stopped but its message could be subverted by planting the seeds of doubt and confusion in the minds of the masses, who would consume the information and false knowledge controlled by the Vatican.

Throughout its history, the Catholic Church has been responsible for forging many documents and manuscripts to help its rise to power. In an attempt to counter the KJV, the false church released its own Bible in 1610, the Douay-Rheims, which was based on the Latin Vulgate. Two allegedly ancient manuscripts, the Codex Vaticanus and the Codex Sinaiticus, have been used by the Vatican to back up their claim to the authentic Word of God, as these manuscripts of Alexandrian descent are significantly different from the Textus Receptus. If these manuscripts could be shown to be older than the Textus Receptus, then doubt would be cast on the validity of the received text; they have been dated to the 4th century and are stated everywhere as being the "oldest and best", and therefore, most reliable, despite overwhelming evidence that they are anything but! Vaticanus is actually a 15th century manuscript, and Sinaiticus was produced in the 19th century by Constantine Simonides, a Greek palaeographer who was an expert in calligraphy and copying ancient documents.[6]

Vaticanus was apparently discovered in the Vatican library in 1475 after going unnoticed for over a thousand years! Evidence points to the fact that it was actually forged in Rome itself, just prior to its "discovery".[7] The Vatican had kept it hidden ever since, but plans were being made to release a facsimile copy to the world as part of a plot to finally discredit the Textus Receptus – which was being translated into many languages and spread around the world by the numerous Bible societies that were springing up everywhere, much to the horror of the Papacy and the Jesuits. If the Vatican could find a second manuscript, one that was in agreement with Vaticanus, then the Church would have a powerful weapon to inflict a lethal blow to the Textus Receptus that had caused so much damage to the Synagogue of Satan.

Codex Sinaiticus was supposedly discovered by Constantin von Tischendorf, a German Biblical scholar, in a wastepaper bin that was being used to feed the fire at St Catherine's Monastery on the Sinai Peninsula. Tischendorf, a Lutheran, had been summoned to an audience with Pope Gregory XVI at the Vatican in 1843, where he became the first Protestant to be granted access to study Codex Vaticanus. He had always been a very vocal critic of the Textus Receptus, which put him on the Jesuits' radar as someone who could be very useful to their cause.

Simonides had been commissioned to produce a copy of an ancient Bible by the Greek Orthodox Church as a gift to the Russian Tsar; this was clearly a ruse, as his work found its way to St Catherine's after being aged and significantly altered. Everything went to plan as Tischendorf was guided to make his "discovery", and after his final visit to Sinai in 1859, he acquired the last of his 346 sheets of parchment and revealed it to the world.

"Coincidentally", this was only two years after the Vatican released its copy of Vaticanus to the public, and the same year that Darwin published his book *On the Origin of Species*, which further undermined the Word of God.

The Christian world fell for the lie despite Simonides going public, revealing that he had produced Sinaiticus. The so-called experts were all too quick to hail the discovery as the "oldest and best" copy of the scriptures, which added weight to the Vatican's claim that Codex Vaticanus was older, and therefore more reliable, than the Protestant Bibles based on the Textus Receptus.

The final stage in this great deception came just over twenty years later, in 1881, when a revision was made to the King James Bible by a committee of charlatans headed by two Cambridge professors: Brook Foss Westcott and Fenton John Anthony Hort. These men shared Tischendorf's hatred of the Textus Receptus and started work on their own Greek text based on the newly revealed, "older and better" Vaticanus and Sinaiticus. Westcott and Hort were both members of the High Church, a branch of the Anglican Church (or Church of England), which shares many of the beliefs and rituals of Catholicism. Purgatory, the Sacraments and Mary worship were all embraced by these men, who also held a strong interest in the Occult, being key members of the Ghostly Guild (or Ghost Club), which investigated supernatural events and contacted the spirits through séances. Hort would go on to become a member of the blasphemous secret society of twelve who called themselves the Cambridge Apostles, swearing a binding oath of silence that was written by Hort himself. The infallibility of the Bible and the Genesis account of Creation were not believed by Westcott and Hort, who felt Darwin's explanation was much more plausible.

Bearing all this is mind, you could not find two worse candidates to be responsible for revising the Protestant King James Bible. "Revision" is probably a bad choice of words, as it was not a revision at all. Wescott and Hort secretly gave their Greek text to the revision committee, and this became the foundation that the new Bible was built upon. The true Word of God that had survived through more than five thousand manuscripts of the Antioch line, which culminated in the Authorised King James Bible, had finally been broken. Rome had inflicted a deadly blow to the Textus Receptus, and from 1881, all of the modern Bibles (including the RSV, NASV, GNB, ESV and NIV) were based on the Alexandrian, Gnostic-inspired line of only forty-five manuscripts, particularly Rome's beloved Vaticanus and Sinaiticus.

The New International Version (NIV) would go on to become the most popular of all the modern translations. Rupert Murdoch, the owner of Zondervan/Harper Collins, published the NIV together with the Satanic Bible, and as a result of his work, he was knighted by the Pope into the Order of St Gregory the Great for his services to Rome – you really couldn't make this up!

After 1881, there has been a steady decline in numbers of those who follow the teachings of the Reformation. Many people still identify as Protestant, but ask them what it is that they are protesting and you will most likely be met by a blank expression and silence. The true answer, which would have been given by all less than 150 years ago, is: "I am protesting the authority of the Pope over the Church, and I denounce him as the Antichrist of Scripture and prophecy."

The Bible that most Christians read today has been massively corrupted as most people have replaced God with science. To the majority, God and the Bible are nothing more than a fairy tale, a crutch that the uneducated people of the past leant on because they didn't have the understanding we have today from people such as Charles Darwin, Stephen Hawking and David Attenborough.

Life on Earth is nothing more than a test, a test that Satan wants us to fail. Satan's sole purpose, through his ambassador on Earth, the Antichrist, is to keep us distracted and fill our minds with false information so that we never seek or find the one true God.

Our purpose in life is to recognise that we have been Created, and to acknowledge and give thanks to our Creator for the gift He has given us. We are to follow the spirit of His moral code, which is fulfilled by loving God with all our heart and soul, and loving our neighbour as ourselves. Finally, we are to believe that Jesus paid the price for the sins we are all guilty of.

God has given all people every opportunity to find Him. His Creation speaks for itself – every plant, tree and animal screams intelligent design if you bother to really think about it – and He left an instruction manual, in the form of the true Bible, that gives all the answers we could ever need.

This life is like the first step of an incredible journey. Pass the test and you will go on to experience things beyond your imagination; fail, and that first step could be your last!

"I call heaven and earth to record this day against you, *that* I have set before you life and death, blessing and cursing; therefore choose life, that both you and your seed may live.

(Deuteronomy 30:19)

1 & 2   Guinness, Henry G., *Romanism and the Reformation*, pp.11–12. J. Nisbet & Co, London. 1891.

3 & 4   White, Ellen G., *The Great Controversy Between Christ and Satan*, Chapter 25: God's Law Immutable. 1888.

5   From its founding, the SDA held many key beliefs that were in direct opposition to Rome, such as rejecting the Trinity, upholding the Seventh Day Sabbath (Saturday) and the traditional Protestant belief that the Pope has always been, and always will be, the Antichrist of Prophecy.

The Jesuit order was founded to destroy the newly emerging threat posed by Protestantism, and one of its main tactics was to infiltrate and overturn the beliefs and teachings of educational institutions, particularly Protestant churches. One of the final beliefs to go from the SDA was the Oneness of God, in the early 20th century, and it is clear that there is a concerted effort to undermine everything else that threatens Rome. New interpretations are creeping into the church that cast doubt on the identification of the Pope as the Antichrist, and the General Council of the SDA are making continual moves towards ecumenism and reconciliation with Rome.

Dr Ganoune Diop is the Director of Public Affairs and Religious Liberty at the SDA world headquarters, and this man has many concerning

connections with Rome, considering the early beliefs of their church. He is listed on, and appears to
be a regular contributor to, the Berkley Center at
the famous Jesuit Georgetown University. From
16–19 October 2018, he attended a conference
at the headquarters of the Jesuit order near the
Vatican, for their "Global Partners" to discuss the
rights of immigrant children. This was nothing
more than a cover to promote the Jesuit's Marxist "Liberation Theology", something that seems
to be gaining momentum today. Dr Ganoune Diop
has also received training at, and earned a PhD
from, the Catholic University of Paris (l'Institut
Catholique de Paris), where many high-ranking
Cardinals of the Church of Rome also trained.

In 1996 the SDA designed a controversial logo
that has been used ever since. Many people have
noticed that the cross that stands upon the open
pages of the Bible appears to be inverted. This accusation has been denied, although the technique
called "negative space" that is incorporated into
the design is very well known and would be no accident. Negative space logos suggest a shape in the
white areas by using dark areas to frame part of
the object being "suggested" – with your brain automatically filling in the missing details. This logo
or "mark" seems to infer the power that now has
influence over and controls the SDA.

6 & 7   Cooper, Bill, *The Forging of Codex Sinaiticus*,
         pp.23–29. Creation Science Movement, 2016.

CHAPTER III

THE LITTLE HORN OF DANIEL VIII

In the previous chapter, we saw how the Little Horn – that Daniel sees in his vision, rising amongst the ten horns on the head of the fourth beast – is a perfect description of the rise of the Papacy after the Western Roman Empire appeared to fall, and that this story is retold in Revelation 13 where the beast (or empire) receives a deadly head wound, which is healed when the Bishop of Rome stands in to fill the power vacuum left by the Caesars.

However, when we come to Daniel's 8th chapter, the chapter that follows this clear description of the rise of the Papal Antichrist, we are faced with a dilemma that has led to a great deal of confusion and debate. Daniel again describes a Little Horn, but this time, his description seems to rule out the Papacy as the one being identified. Why would Daniel describe two different powers as "Little Horns" in back-to-back chapters if he didn't want to confuse his audience?

God is not the author of confusion and He doesn't inspire his Prophets in this regard either. As always, confusion is sown by man's interpretation of Scripture, rather than by

Scripture itself. Quite often, a simple alternative explanation goes unnoticed when the views of trusted commentators are spread and passed down from generation to generation until they are seen on almost the same level as Scripture itself.

The Little Horn of Daniel 8 is a perfect example of this. Daniel starts his chapter describing how Greece defeated the Medo-Persian Empire, which was symbolised by a ram. Greece is seen in his vision as a "he goat" with a notable horn between his eyes. Following its defeat of Medo-Persia, Greece became strong and then the great horn was broken, with four notable ones coming up after it towards the four winds of heaven. The description paints an unmistakable image of Alexander the Great (the first notable horn) and the division of his empire between his four generals following his death (the four notable ones). We then come to verse nine, which is where all the confusion arises. Following Alexander's death and the division of his empire into four regions, we are told,

"And out of one of them came forth a little horn, which waxed exceeding great toward the south, and toward the east, and toward the pleasant land."

For hundreds of years, this verse has been interpreted to mean that a new power would arise out of one of the four divisions of Alexander the Great's empire. By far the most popular opinion points to Antiochus Epiphanes, King of the Seleucid Empire, as being the power in question, although others think it refers to Rome, the empire that followed Greece.

As is so often the case with the Bible, the general consensus is wrong, and I hope to prove that Rome is indeed the Little Horn being spoken of by Daniel in chapter 8, but for very different reasons from those commonly held.

First, let's take a look at the most popular candidate – Antiochus Epiphanes – and show how he cannot be the power being referred to.

Scripture tells us that in the mouth of two or three witnesses shall every word be established. The Bible achieves this by following clear patterns – the same story being told in different ways over many chapters to confirm the narrative. When Daniel was interpreting King Nebuchadnezzar's dream of the great metal man image, he described each consecutive kingdom as getting progressively stronger, starting with Babylon as gold (a soft metal) and ending with Rome as iron (a very strong metal). In Daniel 7, we see Rome being described again as the fourth beast, dreadful and terrible and strong exceedingly. When we come to Daniel's 8th chapter, we see the same pattern and language being used: the ram (Medo-Persia) became great; the he-goat (Greece) became very great; and finally, we see a Little Horn which waxed exceeding great.

Antiochus reigned for just over a decade, was ridiculed as a madman and humiliated by an elderly Roman ambassador, who thwarted Antiochus' plans to capture Egypt and Cyprus by threatening war with the Roman Republic if he didn't capitulate.[1] Antiochus was forced to back down – hardly the action of a man who, supporters of this theory think, the Bible refers to as "exceedingly great", putting him in a more powerful position than both the Medo-Persian Empire and the Greek Empire under Alexander the Great!

The evidence for Antiochus being the Little Horn of Daniel 8 and Daniel 11 – which also describes this power – comes entirely from the book of 1 Maccabees, which is considered canonical Scripture by the Roman Catholic Church but not so by Protestants or any of the main branches of Judaism. 1 Maccabees seems altogether too convenient when it comes to painting Antiochus as the one Daniel sees in his vision; it is as if it were specifically written to tick all the boxes of Daniel 8 and 11, leading the casual reader to only one conclusion.

The book of Daniel tells us many things about this Little Horn power. He would magnify himself, even to the prince of the host, and by him the daily sacrifice was taken away and the place of his sanctuary was cast down. Armies would stand on his part, pollute the sanctuary of strength and place the abomination that makes desolate, casting the truth to the ground, practicing and prospering.

All of these things are spoken of in relation to Antiochus in the book of 1 Maccabees. He ordained that the Israelites should consent to his religion and sacrifice to idols. He forbade burnt offerings, sacrifices and drink offerings in the Temple, that they should profane the Sabbaths and festival days. Altars, groves and chapels of idols were built, and they set up the "Abomination of Desolation" upon the altar, sacrificing swine and unclean beasts to pollute the sanctuary and holy people. From this evidence, it would seem that there is no doubt that Antiochus Epiphanes is the Little Horn power spoken of by the Prophet Daniel – apart from one thing: Jesus Himself totally ruled this out!

Matthew 24, Mark 13 and Luke 21 all describe an event that took place on the Mount of Olives, where Jesus was giving a teaching to His disciples, something that has come to be known as the Olivet Discourse. Upon leaving the Temple, Jesus spoke to His disciples, saying:

"'See you not all these things? Truly I say unto you, there shall not be left here one stone upon another that shall not be thrown down.'

And as he sat upon the Mount of Olives, the disciples came unto him privately saying, 'Tell us, when shall these things be? And what *shall be* the sign of your coming, and of the end of the world?'"

(Matthew 24:2–3)

Jesus was speaking to his disciples in 30AD, just prior to His Crucifixion, and it should be noted that, at this time, all the things He spoke of had not yet come to pass. In Matthew 24:15–16 and Mark 13:14, Jesus warned them that when they should see the "Abomination of Desolation", spoken of by Daniel the Prophet, stand in the Holy place, then those that be in Judea should flee to the mountains. The key to understanding these verses can be found in Luke's gospel, which states:

"And when you shall see Jerusalem compassed with armies, then know that the desolation thereof is near."

(Luke 21:20)

Jesus was being very clear that this would be the "Abomination of Desolation" spoken of by Daniel the Prophet, and it was going to happen exactly forty years after He would be rejected and crucified, fulfilling the sign of Jonah. Antiochus Epiphanes died nearly two hundred years before Jesus gave this warning for the future, completely ruling him out as the one who would place the "Abomination of Desolation"!

We now turn our attention to Rome, the fourth and final beast kingdom upon the Earth, and will show how it perfectly fits the description of the Little Horn power of Daniel 8 and 11.

Following Daniel's description of the "great" Medo-Persian Empire being defeated by the "very great" Greek Empire, we see Greece's great horn being broken and four notable ones "come up" after it. As seen previously, this is a perfect match for the death of Alexander the Great and his empire being divided amongst his four generals: Cassander, Lysimachus, Seleucus and Ptolemy. We then see that "out of one of them came forth a little horn, which waxed exceeding great toward the south, and toward the east, and toward the pleasant land." Scripture follows a pattern, and the Little Horn waxing "exceeding great" is a match with Rome, which is described as "strong exceedingly" in Daniel 7.

Although Rome seems to be a match for the Little Horn power, it is rejected by most commentators for one reason: they can't show how Rome had its origins, that it "came out" of one of the four divisions of Alexander the Great's Empire. For some time, this was a sticking point for me too, as only very tenuous links could be found in this regard, but I still felt that Daniel had to be speaking of Rome; I just couldn't prove it. Then, following a weekly online Bible study with a couple of international friends, where we discussed Daniel's 8th chapter and this problem, I resolved to do an in-depth study in the hope of finding an answer. That evening, everything came together, and I finally found the answer I was seeking.

If Rome's origins were to be found in one of the four divisions of the Greek Empire, I felt it would most likely be in the region closest to Rome, which the map showed to be Macedonia. Macedonia fell under the division ruled by Cassander and was also the place of Alexander the Great's birth.

A simple online search for "Rome and Macedonia" revealed something I wasn't expecting and was a reminder to study every word of Scripture, because misunderstanding just one tiny word can change your interpretation completely.

When the newly emerging power of Rome started to turn its attention towards the Greek Empire, Macedonia was the first to be conquered, and Rome made it the first province of the New Roman Republic in 146BC.[2] From there, Rome "went out" to conquer lands to the south, to the east and toward the pleasant land, just as Daniel had prophesied.

When the Papacy was described in Daniel 7, it was seen as a "little horn" because it was a newly emerging power that "came up" amongst the ten horns, or divisions of the Pagan Roman Empire following the fall of the Caesars. When Alexander died, four notable horns "came up" to replace him and "out of one of them, came forth" the Little Horn. It should be noted that when Daniel describes the rise of the Papacy and of Alexander's four generals, he uses the term "came up" because their origins were in the areas being spoken of, but when he talks of the Little Horn in Daniel 8, he sees it "coming out and going forth". This is a very subtle difference, but it has led people down a false trail for centuries; Daniel never actually implied that this Little Horn, or newly emerging power, had its origins in one of the divisions of Alexander's Empire; we just thought he did and read something into the text that wasn't actually there.

Daniel describes exactly what he saw in the vision. He watches Medo-Persia being defeated by Greece, followed by Greece being divided into four regions controlled by Alexander's generals. Finally, he watches a new power, the Little

Horn, "coming out" of Macedonia, which it had just conquered, and going forth to wax exceeding great toward the south, the east and the pleasant land. Daniel continues to tell how this power would take away the daily sacrifice, place the abomination that makes desolate, pollute the sanctuary of strength and cast it down. We shall see how the Jews continued to sacrifice after they had stoned Steven at the end of Daniel's 70th week; this was the transgression of desolation when God pronounced the sentence upon them. The Abomination of Desolation was the surrounding of Jerusalem by the armies of Pagan Rome just prior to destroying it and leaving it desolate. This was the sentence being carried out at the appointed time, just as Jesus had warned, and exactly forty years after he was rejected and crucified.

Jesus plainly tells us about the Abomination of Desolation, and as Daniel gives more details in his 11th chapter, he paints a perfect picture of the historical rise of the fourth beast kingdom: both Pagan, then Papal, Rome. The people who know their God shall fall by the sword and by flame, by captivity and by spoil, many days. Think here of the persecution of Christians by Pagan Rome all the way through to the Papal inquisitions.

"And the king shall do according to his will; and he shall exalt himself, and magnify himself above every god, and shall speak marvellous things against the God of gods, and shall prosper till the indignation be accomplished; for that that is determined shall be done."

(Daniel 11:36)

This verse is a perfect match for the Little Horn of Daniel 7, which exactly describes the rise and fall of the Papal Antichrist.

"He shall speak *great* words against the most High." (7:25)

"[...] the same horn made war with the saints and prevailed against them,

Until the Ancient of days came, and judgment was given to the saints." (7:21-22)

This Little Horn, as described in Daniel 11, would not regard God nor the desire of women but would magnify himself above all. He would honour the god of forces (Satan) with gold and silver, and with precious stones, and he would divide the land for gain. No better description could be made of the arrogance, opulence and greed of the Papacy.

There was no confusion when Daniel described the Little Horn; in both cases, he was describing the same power: the fourth and final beast kingdom upon Earth. In his 7th chapter, he described the emergence of the final phase of this beast, and in his 8th chapter, he looks back to its rise. The reader is left with a choice: will you put your faith in the words of Jesus and the big picture of world history prophesied by Daniel, or will you follow the world and put your trust in the apocryphal book of 1 Maccabees that is endorsed by the Synagogue of Satan?

Choose wisely!

1 Polybius, *The Histories Vol 6*, book 29, chapter 27, verses 1–8. Loeb Classical Library, Cambridge, MA. 1927.

2 'Macedonian Wars' – Article by the editors of the Encyclopaedia Britannica. Britannica.com.

CHAPTER IV

THE 2300-DAY PROPHECY OF DANIEL VIII AND THE 1260-YEAR REIGN OF THE ANTICHRIST

The 2300-day prophecy of Daniel's 8th chapter is most closely associated with William Miller and the Seventh Day Adventist Church. In 1818, after studying the prophecies in Daniel 8 and 9, Miller came to the conclusion that Christ's Second Coming would be in the year 1843 or 1844. When 1844 passed and it became obvious that Christ was not then returning, the event came to be known as the Great Disappointment.

Rather than admit the mistake, further studies were done, and it was decided that the "Cleansing of the Sanctuary", previously thought to mean the cleansing of the Earth when Jesus returned, was in fact the cleansing of the "Heavenly Sanctuary" instead. This enabled the Adventists to stick to their original date, and the doctrine of "Investigative Judgement" was born, leading to the founding of the SDA.

Miller arrived at the date 1843/44 by adding 2300 years to the starting point of Daniel's 70-week prophecy, which was when King Artaxerxes gave his command to restore and rebuild Jerusalem in 458BC. So where did he go wrong, and is there another explanation? As always, a close reading of Scripture gives the answer.

"Then I heard one saint speaking, and another saint said unto that certain *saint* which spoke, 'How long *shall* be the vision *concerning* the daily *sacrifice* and the transgression of desolation, to give both the sanctuary and the host to be trodden under foot?'

And he said unto me, 'Unto two thousand and three hundred days; then shall the sanctuary be cleansed."

(Daniel 8:13–14)

Daniel's 70-week (or 490-year) prophecy covers several aspects. 70 weeks of years are determined upon his people and the Holy City to finish the transgression, make an end of sins and make reconciliation for iniquity; a commandment would go out to restore and rebuild Jerusalem, and after 69 weeks (or 483 years), Messiah would come. In the midst of the 70th and final week, He would cause the sacrifice and oblation to cease, and would confirm the Covenant with many until the end of the week. The overspreading of abominations would result in the City's and the Sanctuary's destruction, leaving it desolate until the consummation.

When Daniel is given the 2300-day/year prophecy, only a small part of the 70-week prophecy is mentioned, and this, I believe, is where Miller went wrong. The part being discussed in the vision of Daniel 8:13 concerned the daily sacrifice and the transgression of desolation; in other words, the second half of the 70th week, which is the three and a half years between Christ's Crucifixion in 30AD and the stoning of Steven in 33AD, which ended the 490 years.

Miller took his starting date from the beginning of the 70 weeks rather than the end of it. The transgression of desolation occurred in 33 AD when the Jews failed to make an end of sins and reconciliation for iniquity; Steven gave them a final opportunity to finish the transgression and bring everlasting righteousness by repenting and accepting that their Messiah had come. Therefore, 33 AD has to be the starting point, because the 2300-day/year prophecy would not have come into effect if the Jews had taken their chance to end the transgression. Because, instead, they killed Steven and continued the daily sacrifice, this became the overspreading of abominations, the transgression of desolation, to make both the Sanctuary and the host be trodden under foot for 2300 years until the Sanctuary would be cleansed by Christ's return.

If this is the correct understanding, it means that the consummation and Christ's return will be in the year 2333. Many people have set dates for Christ's return, just as William Miller did, and it is rightly pointed out that Jesus stated:

"But of that day and hour knows no *man*, no, not the angels of heaven, but my Father only."

(Matthew 24:36)

It is not my intention to date set, but time prophecies are given for a reason, and if they couldn't be worked out then what purpose would they serve? Daniel studied Jeremiah's prophecy and worked out that the Jewish captivity would be coming to an end, and we can see how the prophecy given by Gabriel to Daniel accurately pointed to the year that Messiah would arrive. If new information is uncovered that shows Scripture identifying a time period for Christ's return, this shouldn't be dismissed for fear of date setting. Not knowing the day or the hour speaks of a precise time, but Scripture says nothing about not being able to work out the year!

At the time of writing, this event is potentially only 312 years away, so is that plausible? If anything, considering the state the world is in and the extreme level of deception we are living under, the only surprise is that we have that long!

Whilst researching the chapter on the Antichrist at the start of this book, an amazing coincidence stood out that may well be a second witness to confirm this date theory. Daniel's 7th chapter describes a Little Horn rising out of the head of the fourth beast, and the New Testament identifies this person as the Man of Sin, the Son of Perdition, the false prophet or, to use his most well-known title, the Antichrist. There are several features or stages that point to who this person is.

He is revealed when the power that was ruling in Paul's day was taken out of the way. This occurred in 476AD when the Western Roman Empire appeared to fall, and Caesar was replaced by the Bishop of Rome, who filled the power vacuum that they left. It was during this time that we saw the great falling away spoken of by Paul in his second letter to the Thessalonians, where many false doctrines entered into the Church that was now controlled by Rome. This was the first stage in the rise to power of the Antichrist.

He would grow in power amongst the ten horns (or kingdoms) that the Western Empire divided into after the fall of the Caesars. These kingdoms had already converted to Christianity, so they looked to the Bishop of Rome, as head of the Church, for spiritual recognition.

Three horns (or kingdoms) would be plucked up by the roots before he would reach full power and authority. These three were the Vandals in 534AD, the Ostrogoths in 552AD and, finally, Charlemagne's defeat of the Lombards in 774AD, which led to the emergence of the Papal States and the temporal power of the Pope.

Paul states that this man would:

"[...] oppose and exalt himself above all that is called God or that is worshipped, so that he, as God, sits in the temple of God, showing himself that he is God."

(2 Thessalonians 2:4)

Only the Papacy fulfils all of these conditions perfectly. The Bishop of Rome revealed the Man of Sin when he replaced Caesar, before growing in power amongst the ten divided nations of the Western Roman Empire, until Emperor Phocas made Boniface III the last Bishop and the first Pope of Rome in 607AD.

The year 774AD saw the third horn being plucked up by the roots, and 300 years later, a significant change occurred that announced the full power of the Antichrist had been realised. In 1073AD, Hildebrand was elected as Pope Gregory VII and announced a theocracy on Earth, claiming that, as the representative of deity, he was to be above all the kings of the world.[1] He took all spiritual power from the control of the state and gained complete independence. He excommunicated Henry IV, the German Emperor, releasing his subjects from obeying or having allegiance to him. The Pope then asserted that the election of all bishops in the Catholic Church had to be confirmed by him, which took the power from the churches to appoint their own bishops and placed it in the hands of a foreign entity, the Papacy.[2]

Both Daniel and John in the book of Revelation state that the Antichrist will be given power to wear out the Saints for 1260 years, with Revelation 13:5 giving a key extra detail when it says:

"And there was given unto him a mouth speaking great things and blasphemies, and power was given unto him to continue forty-two months."

The word "continue" is very important because the vast majority of commentators start the 1260-year reign from either the decree of Justinian or the decree of Phocas, which means that the 1260-year reign of the Antichrist would have ended at least 150 years ago, despite all the evidence showing that he is still very much in control. The most logical starting point for the Antichrist to have been given, to continue for 1260 years, would be when he claimed to be as God on Earth, having power over kings and emperors. When Gregory VII became Pope in 1073AD, Paul's prophecy (as recorded in 2 Thessalonians 2:4) was fulfilled with Gregory assuming absolute power on Earth – and this is where things get really interesting. If you add 1260 years to 1073AD, you come to 2333AD, exactly the same year you come to when you add 2300 years to the end of Daniel's 70th week in 33AD, when the Jews failed to end the transgression. Is this a huge coincidence or something more? Only time will tell!

2300 DAYS / YEARS

DANIEL 8:13-14

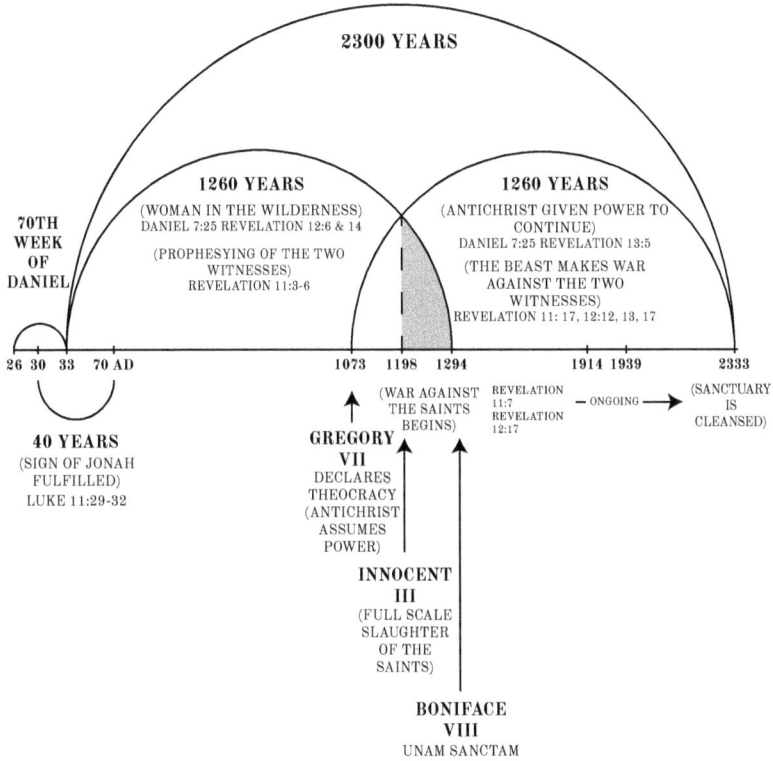

2300 YEARS

70TH WEEK OF DANIEL

1260 YEARS
(WOMAN IN THE WILDERNESS)
DANIEL 7:25 REVELATION 12:6 & 14

(PROPHESYING OF THE TWO WITNESSES)
REVELATION 11:3-6

1260 YEARS
(ANTICHRIST GIVEN POWER TO CONTINUE)
DANIEL 7:25 REVELATION 13:5

(THE BEAST MAKES WAR AGAINST THE TWO WITNESSES)
REVELATION 11: 17, 12:12, 13, 17

26 30 33   70 AD   1073 1198 1294   1914 1939   2333

40 YEARS
(SIGN OF JONAH FULFILLED)
LUKE 11:29-32

(WAR AGAINST THE SAINTS BEGINS)

REVELATION 11:7
REVELATION 12:17

— ONGOING →

(SANCTUARY IS CLEANSED)

GREGORY VII DECLARES THEOCRACY (ANTICHRIST ASSUMES POWER)

INNOCENT III (FULL SCALE SLAUGHTER OF THE SAINTS)

BONIFACE VIII UNAM SANCTAM

1   D'Aubigné, Jean-Henri M., *History of the Reformation of The Sixteenth Century*, pp.12–13. Oliver & Boyd, London. 1847.

2   'Dictatus Papae' (Dictates of the Pope). Pope Gregory's 27 declarations of Papal supremacy (1075AD).

CHAPTER V

THE 1290- AND 1335-DAY PROPHECY OF DANIEL XII

"And from the time *that* the daily *sacrifice* shall be taken away, and the abomination that makes desolate set up, *there shall be* a thousand two hundred and ninety days.

Blessed *is* he that waits and comes to the thousand, three hundred and five and thirty days."

(Daniel 12:11–12)

I spent countless hours over many months trying to make sense of these two verses from the final chapter of Daniel, but nothing seemed to fit. With this being a prophecy, we have to follow the day-for-a-year principle as used throughout Daniel's book.

The daily sacrifice was taken away and the abomination that makes desolate set up in 70AD when the 10th Legion of General Titus began the siege of Jerusalem during Passover of that year, leading to its destruction. If we take 70AD as the starting point and add 1290 years, we come to the year 1360AD. Then, a further 45 years, or 1335 in total, brings us to 1405AD. Nothing about these dates revealed anything significant, and how could anyone wait until 1335 years are over? Nothing about this made any sense.

Some people try to get around this problem by making the time periods literal days, and either assign them to a period in the distant past, or place them in the future with a revived sacrificial system, in a rebuilt third temple, being taken away. This futurist interpretation comes from the Jesuits' attempt to hide the fact that it was Jesus who fully fulfilled Daniel's 70th week, as described in Daniel 9:24–27.

Jesus said that if you "ask, it shall be given you; seek and you shall find" (Matthew 7:7). I always knew that the answer I was seeking would be within Scripture; it was just a matter of making the right connections with guidance from the Holy Spirit. I often prayed for help and understanding regarding these verses, and one day, everything seemed to fall into place.

It's very easy to get caught up reading the same verse over and over again, unable to see past the teachings given by others. These teachings can blind us to what has actually been written and the context it should be taken in. With this prophecy, context is everything, as it reveals the hidden meaning that has been completely overlooked.

Virtually all scholars agree that Daniel is a parallel book to Revelation, and this is our first clue. Daniel's book gives us an overview of the four great kingdoms/empires upon the Earth, with an emphasis on Babylon, the first kingdom, whereas Revelation concentrates on the fourth and final kingdom, Rome. Daniel's 2nd and 7th chapters give a brief description of this final kingdom and its prophesied downfall, but Revelation goes into great detail about it, revealing things that were hidden from Daniel.

The book of Revelation ends with the destruction of the fourth beast kingdom which, in its final phase, is controlled by the Papal Antichrist. After it is destroyed, Christ returns to set up His kingdom that shall be without end, the stone cut out without hands, which is thus described by Daniel: "that smote the image and became a great mountain that filled the whole earth." (2:35) This is our second clue.

The context of Daniel's final chapter relates to the end times. It starts with him being told about a time of trouble such as the Earth has never seen, followed by the resurrection of the Saints in verses 2 and 3. Daniel is then told to shut up the book until the time of the end. He goes on to hear two men, one asking the other, "How long shall it be to the end of these wonders?" The other tells the first "that it shall be for a time, times, and a half; and when he shall have accomplished to scatter the power of the holy people, all these things shall be finished." This statement prophesied the coming 1260-year reign of the Antichrist Popes and the wearing out of the Saints, or "Holy People". Daniel doesn't understand this and asks his Lord (most likely Gabriel), "What shall be the end of these things?" He is told, "Go your way, for the words are closed up and sealed till the time of the end." Daniel is deliberately given vague information because the prophecy was for the end times and its revelation was not something that he should concern himself with.

When we take a close look at the 1290 and 1335 days/years, it's important to note that the prophecy states "from" the time that the daily sacrifice is taken away "and" the abomination that makes desolate set up. "From" can also be read as "after", so this is speaking of a time after the destruction of Jerusalem and its Temple, which took away the sacrificial system, and the setting up of the time of desolation. In the previous chapter, we saw how the 2300 years of desolation would occur as a direct result of the Jews' failure to finish the transgression at the end of Daniel's 70th week in 33AD. So, this period of desolation refers to the appointed period of time that God would turn his back on the Jewish nation to allow them to suffer punishment at the hands of their enemies.

With this understanding, and taking into account the context of the chapter, we can see from Scripture that the time following Jerusalem's destruction and decreed period of desolation is the millennial reign of Christ. We all know that Christ's millennial reign of peace on Earth lasts for 1000 years, so how does this relate to the 1290 and 1335 years of Daniel 12:11–12?

The book of Revelation provides us the key to unlock this prophecy, with chapter 20 providing the missing details. After the battle of Armageddon, when the Antichrist's kingdom is destroyed, Satan is bound and cast into the bottomless pit for 1000 years:

"[...] that he should deceive the nations no more, till the thousand years should be fulfilled; and after that he must be loosed a little season."

(Revelation 20:3)

During the 1000 years, the Saints who make up the first resurrection live and reign with Christ over the remnant of nations who survived Armageddon.

"Blessed and holy *is* he that has part in the first resurrection. On such the second death has no power, but they shall be priests of God and of Christ, and shall reign with him a thousand years."

(Revelation 20:6)

This is our third clue because it is the same as the language used in Daniel 12:12, which states, "Blessed is he that waits and comes to the thousand, three hundred and five and thirty days." Obviously, no mortal human could wait until 1335 years had elapsed, but if this is speaking of the Saints who will be part of the first resurrection, then it would be entirely possible, as they will be immortal and the second death will have no power over them.

So, to break this down, we will have the 1000-year reign of Christ and the Saints, followed by Satan being given a period of time to deceive the nations once more and gather them together against Jerusalem. Revelation 20:8 tells us how Satan will be released from his prison:

"And shall go out to deceive the nations which are in the four quarters of the earth, Gog and Magog, to gather them together to battle, the number of whom is as the sand of the sea."

This period could well last for 290 years, bringing us to the 1290 years described in Daniel's prophecy.

Throughout history, we see how nations have completely turned around from morally good behaviour to the exact opposite in a period of about 300 years. In England, Henry VIII started the Protestant Church of England, separating from Rome in 1534. Then, 300 years later, in 1833, the Oxford Movement began, which reintroduced Catholic doctrine into the Church, marking the beginning of the downfall of Protestantism in England.

The Pilgrim Fathers travelled from England to America, establishing the Plymouth colony in Massachusetts in 1620. This exodus to the New World aimed to set up a pure Christian lifestyle, but 300 years later we saw the "roaring '20s", with complete decadence replacing the Pilgrims' dreams of a heaven on Earth.

If the 1290 years refers to the millennial reign followed by Satan deceiving the nations for 290 years, then what about the 1335 years, which adds forty-five years to the 1290?

Revelation 20:9 explains how after the nations had been deceived:

"They went up on the breadth of the earth, and compassed the camp of the Saints about and the beloved city: and fire came down from God out of heaven and devoured them."

The Prophet Ezekiel also described how Gog and Magog would come to war against the Saints, saying:

"'And you shall come up against my people of Israel, as a cloud to cover the land; it shall be in the latter days, and I will bring you against my land, that the heathen may know me, when I shall be sanctified in you, O Gog, before their eyes.'"

(Ezekiel 38:16)

He goes on to describe God's vengeance upon Gog and the fire and brimstone that will rain down upon him and his army, as previously described in Revelation 20:9.

Following the destruction of Gog and Magog, we are told that the house of Israel shall be burying the dead for seven months to cleanse the land:

"'And they that dwell in the cities of Israel shall go forth and shall set on fire and burn the weapons, both the shields and the bucklers, the bows and the arrows, and the hand-staves, and the spears; and they shall burn them with fire seven years."

(Ezekiel 39:9)

The gathering together of the nations for this final great battle, together with the aftermath described by Ezekiel, could well account for the remaining forty-five years, which would bring us to the 1335. Blessed and holy is he that comes to this time, because what follows is the Great White Throne Judgment where the second death will have no power over him. As previously stated, Daniel is a parallel book to Revelation, so it makes perfect sense for his last chapter to be foretelling the events described at the end of Revelation. After being given this last time prophecy, Daniel is told, "Go your way till the end be; for you shall rest, and stand in the lot at the end of the days." (12:13) This is our final clue.

Daniel doesn't really understand, because the words are closed up and sealed till the time of the end, but the book of Revelation gives the key to Daniel's message. He is being told to get on with his life until he shall rest in the grave; then, that when the current age comes to an end, he will be resurrected to stand in his allotted place, to live and reign with Christ for 1000 years; then to wait until the 1335 years are complete before he gains his reward in the New Jerusalem, the Eternal Kingdom that shall be without end.

CHAPTER VI

THE SEVEN SEALS OF REVELATION

Everyone has heard of the four horsemen of the Apocalypse, who make up the first four of the seven seals of Revelation chapter 6, but who or what do they represent? The common understanding is that they are symbolic of conquest, war, famine and death, all things that are expected to occur during the time of tribulation that will precede Christ's Second Coming.

As is so often the case, interpretations from respected scholars that appear to fit are passed down and accepted as fact, so people no longer see or question the text being read, having absorbed the understanding of others.

I only became a Christian in 2016, when I was forty-six years old, after God revealed His existence to me in ways I couldn't deny. I had always been quite obsessive when it came to researching a subject that took my interest, so when my life was turned upside-down by the understanding that the Bible is in fact true, I put these skills to good use and became totally absorbed in the scriptures. It didn't take me long to realise that many of the doctrines and traditions that are followed by mainstream Christianity are actually false and in direct opposition to the gospel teachings.

I really wanted to become part of a community of like-minded people, but it quickly became apparent that if I wanted to worship God in spirit and in truth, it would not be found in the churches, but in Scripture itself. Without having a previous understanding of Christianity, apart from the very basics, I was able to read the Bible without any preconceived ideas. I realise now what an advantage this has been, as it's incredibly difficult to read Scripture impartially if you have had the ideas of others drummed into you from an early age.

When I came to the 6th chapter of Revelation, something stood out immediately to me. The book of Daniel was still fresh in my mind, so when I read about the four horses and the riders that controlled them, I was reminded of the four beast kingdoms and the kings who ruled them, as described in Daniel 7. This chapter, which tells us of Daniel's dream, is also an expansion of King Nebuchadnezzar's dream, who saw the same four kingdoms but represented by a great image or statue that comprised of four sections, each being made from a different metal. Could it be that the four horsemen of the Apocalypse are actually representations of the four beast kingdoms of Babylon, Medo-Persia, Greece and Rome?

Many people have noticed that Daniel and Revelation appear to be parallel books, but the connection between the horsemen and the beast kingdoms seems to have been overlooked. The more I studied, the more I became convinced that Revelation 6–22 actually represents a retelling of the events described in Daniel chapters 2 and 7.

In Revelation 5:1–9, John is given a vision of heaven, with God seated on His throne, holding a book sealed with seven seals. An angel proclaims, "Who is worthy to open the book and to loose the seals thereof?" John is then shown Jesus, who appears as a lamb as if it had been slain, and is told that He had prevailed to open the book and loose the seals because He was slain and had redeemed them to God by his blood.

It is widely taught that the opening of the seven seals unleashes plagues upon the Earth during the end times, to punish the wicked before Christ's return. There are many problems with this theory, as we shall see later, but it will become clear that they actually represent seven stages of Earth's history, from Babylon, the first world kingdom/empire, to the Second Coming of Christ to establish His kingdom that shall endure forever. If the four horsemen in fact represent the four beast kingdoms, then there would have to be similarities with Daniel's description of them, and this is precisely what we find.

When the first seal is opened, we:

"[...] behold a white horse, and he that sat on him had a bow, and a crown was given unto him, and he went forth conquering, and to conquer."

(Revelation 6:2)

Babylon was the first world kingdom as described by Daniel the Prophet. King Nebuchadnezzar is told by Daniel that:

"You, O king, *are* a king of kings. for the God of heaven has given you a kingdom, power, and strength, and glory;

and wheresoever the children of men dwell, the beasts of the field and the fowls of the heaven has he given into your hand, and has made you ruler over them all."

(Daniel 2:37–38)

The opening of the second seal sees:

"[...] another horse *that was* red; and *power* was given to him that sat thereon to take peace from the earth, and that they should kill one another; and there was given unto him a great sword."

(Revelation 6:4)

Medo-Persia was the second world kingdom described in Daniel's prophecy. When King Belshazzar, Nebuchadnezzar's son, became prideful and failed to glorify God, he was slain, and his kingdom given to the Medes and the Persians. The relative peace of the first world kingdom was taken away and a new power now prevailed. (See also Jeremiah 29:4–7.)

Daniel's dream saw this second kingdom represented by:

"[...] a bear, and it raised up itself on one side, and *it had* three ribs in the mouth of it between the teeth of it, and they said thus into it: 'Arise, devour much flesh.'"

(Daniel 7:5)

The Medo-Persian Empire achieved its power through military strength, defeating Babylon, Lydia and Egypt, the three ribs in the bear's mouth, hence, "there was given unto him a great sword".

When the third seal is opened, we see:

"[...] a black horse, and he that sat on him had a pair of balances in his hand.

And I heard a voice in the midst of the four beasts say, 'A measure of wheat for a penny, and three measures of barley for a penny, and *see* you hurt not the oil and the wine.'"

(Revelation 6:5-6)

This third seal is the most difficult of the four to decipher as its language is very cryptic, so we can only speculate as

to its precise meaning. Greece was the third world kingdom
that Daniel described, so how does the third horseman of
Revelation fit in with what we have just read?

Ancient Greece was known for philosophy and natural
law, where man's wisdom was celebrated over the Word and
law of God. The instruction to not hurt the oil and the wine
may well have been a warning not to corrupt the faith of
the Church through false doctrine and man-made ideas. The
true Church is symbolised by a natural olive tree made up of
Jewish believers in Christ, together with Gentile believers
(the wild olive branches) that have been grafted in through
faith (Romans 11:11–24). Lampstands are also symbolic of
the Church (Revelation 1:20), and it is oil (or faith) that
feeds the lampstand (or Church), enabling it to burn brightly, giving light to the world (Leviticus 24:2). Wine symbolises good doctrine, which strengthens the Church, allowing
it to bear fruit.

The false doctrine of the Trinity was born out of Greek
philosophy, where Platonic ideas regarding the triune nature
of God were absorbed by the Church of Rome, who then
forced this doctrine upon the Christian world. One measure
of wheat equalling a penny and three measures of barley
having the same value could be a reference to the Trinity,
with man's so-called wisdom corrupting the understanding
of the true nature of God.

"And when he had opened the fourth seal, I heard the
voice of the fourth beast say, 'Come and see.'

And I looked, and behold a pale horse, and his name that
sat on him was Death, and Hell followed with him. And power was given unto them over the fourth part of the earth, to

kill with sword, and with hunger, and with death, and with the beasts of the earth."

(Revelation 6:7–8)

Rome was the fourth world kingdom, and its description by Daniel is a perfect match for the rider of the pale horse. He beholds:

"[...] a fourth beast, dreadful and terrible and strong exceedingly; and it had great iron teeth; it devoured and broke in pieces, and stamped the residue with the feet of it."

(Daniel 7:7)

This fourth kingdom did indeed kill with the sword and also with the living creatures of the Earth, the most obvious example being the feeding of Christians to the lions and other wild animals for entertainment in the Colosseum.

During the research for this chapter, I received confirmation from a completely unexpected source regarding this final horseman having power over the fourth part of the Earth. I had the television on in the background and I heard a movie starting, so I waited to see if it was anything worth watching. It turned out that the film in question was *Gladiator*, and during the opening scene, some text came up on screen to give context to what was about to be shown. This text immediately got my attention and read as follows:

"At the height of its power, the Roman Empire was vast, stretching from the deserts of Africa to the borders of northern England. Over one quarter of the world's population lived and died under the rule of the Caesars."

God really does work in mysterious ways, and this extra bit of information gave me added reassurance that I was on the right track.

After the description of the four beast kingdoms upon the Earth, Daniel goes on to describe another power (the Little Horn) that rises out of the fourth kingdom of Rome, and how it would make war with the Saints of the Most High and prevail against them until a time, times and the dividing of time (Daniel 7:21 & 25).

When the fifth seal is opened, John:

"[...] saw under the altar, the souls of them that were slain for the word of God, and for the testimony which they held.

And they cried with a loud voice, saying, 'How long, O LORD, holy and true, do you not judge and avenge our blood on them that dwell on the earth?'

And white robes were given unto every one of them, and it was said unto them, that they should rest yet for a little season, until their fellow servants also, and their brethren that should be killed as they *were*, should be fulfilled."

(Revelation 6:9–11)

Daniel's description of the new power that emerges from Rome to make war with the Saints mirrors John's description of the souls under the altar who are waiting for God to avenge their blood. The fifth seal clearly covers a great many years, with the dead getting impatient as they wait for God to bring them justice. It should be remembered that the book of Revelation describes John's vision, where he sees the future, symbolically. The dead "crying out" is not to be understood literally as they have no sense of consciousness whatsoever until they are resurrected; this description is designed to show the long period of time from the first martyrs of Jesus until the consummation.

Daniel foresaw that the war against the Saints would last for 1260 years, the length of time that the Little Horn Antichrist power would reign, before being brought to an end by the return of Christ. The souls under the altar would have to wait until the 1260 years are fulfilled so their brethren, who would also suffer as they did, could join them. As seen in the previous chapters, the 1260 years that the Antichrist was given to "continue" began in 1073 AD when Hildebrand ascended the Chair of St Peter. With this understanding, it can be seen that the Antichrist's reign and his war against the Saints is not yet over, so many more souls are yet to join their brethren.

We are currently living in the latter stages of the fifth seal as the sixth has not yet been opened; therefore, the four horsemen of the Apocalypse have already ridden and cannot represent the end times plagues upon the Earth.

The opening of the sixth seal brings:

"[...] a great earthquake, and the sun became black as sackcloth of hair, and the moon became as blood.

And the stars of heaven fell unto the earth, even as a fig tree casts her untimely figs when she is shaken of a mighty wind."

(Revelation 6:12–13)

Daniel gives us a very condensed overview of Earth's history, beginning in Babylon, without the details we read about later in the Revelation. The reign of the Antichrist and his coming destruction is summed up in a few short verses, but we are left in no doubt as to his identity. The sixth seal brings signs in the heavens and on Earth to announce that the great day of the wrath of the Lamb is about to begin. Daniel doesn't really speak of this stage because it was most likely seen as an unnecessary detail at the time he was given his dream, which served to highlight the four beast kingdoms and their eventual destruction.

The synoptic gospels of Matthew, Mark and Luke accurately describe this stage when Jesus Himself states:

"'Immediately after the tribulation of those days shall the sun be darkened, and the moon shall not give her light, and the stars shall fall from heaven, and the powers of the heavens shall be shaken.'"

(Matthew 24:29)

This is a direct reference to the sixth seal, with the signs occurring before Christ's return but after the Papal persecutions of the fifth seal.

Finally, we come to the opening of the seventh seal, and there is silence in heaven before the seven trumpets are sounded and the seven vials poured out that represent God's final judgement upon the Earth. When the last trumpet is heard, the Saints of Christ are raised to meet him in the air, first the dead, quickly followed by those still living, before the final judgements bring us to "the consummation, and that determined shall be poured out upon the desolate." (Daniel 9:27)

The sixth and seventh vials mark the end of the world as we know it, when the great battle of Armageddon will destroy the Wicked, with the Antichrist and his kingdom consumed in the lake of fire. Yet again, Daniel 2 and 7 are in perfect harmony with Revelation's seventh seal, when we see the stone that strikes the image becoming a mountain that fills the whole Earth, which symbolises the return of the Son of Man, who is given a kingdom that shall endure forever and never be destroyed (Daniel 2:34–35 & 7:13–14).

CHAPTER VII

THE SEVEN KINGS OF REVELATION XVII

There is much debate as to the identity of the seven kings of Revelation 17. Some say that they are either seven Roman emperors or seven forms of Roman government, whilst others think that it refers to seven Popes. To make sense of this, we have to consult the book of Daniel, which is the parallel book to Revelation; as is often the case, when faced with a difficult verse or teaching in one book, the answer can be found in its twin.

The context of Revelation 17 is a description of the Great Whore, Mystery, Babylon the Great, the Woman arrayed in purple and scarlet colour who is drunk with the blood of the Saints. We have previously identified this Woman as the false church of Rome, with the Antichrist Popes at its head.

In John's vision, the angel tells him the mystery of the Woman, and of the beast that carries her, which has seven heads and ten horns. He is told that the beast was, and is not, and shall ascend out of the bottomless pit, and go into perdition. Revelation 20:2–3 gives the identity of the beast as the Devil and Satan, who ascends from the bottomless pit to deceive the nations again, after first being bound for 1000 years upon Christ's return. John is told that:

"The seven heads are seven mountains, on which the woman sits.

And there are seven kings. Five are fallen, and one is, *and* the other is not yet come; and when he comes, he must continue a short space.

And the beast that was, and is not, even he is the eighth, and is of the seven, and goes into perdition."

(Revelation 17:9–11)

Rome has always been known as the City of the Seven Hills, and the Catholic Church is the Woman that rides or controls this scarlet-coloured beast. To find the identity of the seven kings, we need to go back to Daniel chapters 2 and 7. In Daniel's second chapter, he interprets King Nebuchadnezzar's dream and tells him that the sections of the great image that the king saw represented four kingdoms upon the Earth, and that in the days of these "kings" shall the God of heaven set up a kingdom which shall never be destroyed.

Daniel goes on to have his own dream about these four kingdoms, and instead of them being represented by sections of an image made up of different metals, Daniel's dream is more detailed and sees them as four great beasts.

The first beast (or king) represented Babylon and was seen as a lion with eagle's wings.

The second beast was like a bear, raised up on one side with three ribs in its mouth.

The third beast was like a leopard with four wings and four heads.

The fourth was a dreadful and terrible beast with great iron teeth, and it had ten horns.

These world kingdoms or empires had seven heads between them, each one representing a king. When Rome came to power, it was not identified as any known beast because it was a composite of all the previous kingdoms, taking on aspects of each (as seen in Revelation 13:2). It is described as like a leopard, but with the feet of a bear and the mouth of a lion.

The Roman beast had seven heads, one representing the Babylonian king (lion), one representing the Medo-Persian king (bear), four representing the Greek kings (leopard), and its own head, the seventh.

Now that we know that the seven kings represent the four great kingdoms upon the Earth, the pieces start falling into place. The obvious starting point is the king that the angel describes as "the one that is". In John's day, the power that had control was the Pagan Roman Empire under the Caesars, symbolised by the king that is.

Then, counting backwards, we have "five that are fallen". Immediately before Rome, Greece was the kingdom that fell, represented by four heads (or kings). Before Greece, we had Medo-Persia, which was another head (or king), so Greece and Medo-Persia are the five that are fallen.

The obvious question remaining is: what about Babylon? The reason for Babylon being left out of the count will become apparent very soon.

After the Pagan Roman Empire, we have another king that "is not yet come, and when he comes, he must continue a short space." In 312AD, Emperor Constantine allegedly converted to Christianity, and the following year he legalised the new religion throughout the Roman Empire. Although he labelled himself a Christian, Constantine continued his Pagan traditions and beliefs until his death. Under Constantine, the false doctrine of the Trinity was instituted, and Sunday, the venerable day of the sun, was legislated to be a day of rest for all citizens, a replacement Sabbath, that put them back under the law.

When the Roman Empire realised that Christianity could not be stopped, it decided that its survival would only be ensured if it became the head of this new religion; thus, a beast started to rise out of the sea – Rome, morphing and reinventing itself on the surface as a Christian empire, whilst under the surface and at its heart it was still as Pagan as ever. The gods of Pagan Rome became the Saints of the Universal or Catholic Church, and an image started to form that would cause the world to worship the beast.

John sees this beast in Revelation 13 as having seven heads with ten horns and ten crowns upon the horns, and upon his heads, the name of blasphemy. In Revelation 12, there were only seven crowns upon the beast, and these were on the heads; this symbolised the Pagan Roman Empire at the time of Christ, when all the power was with the Empire, which, as previously seen, was a combination of all the empires that preceded it.

The change in Revelation 13's sea beast sees the crowns moving from the heads onto the horns, which was foretelling the coming dissolution of the Western Empire, with power shifting to the ten individual regions that it separated into. This beast is given its power, throne and great authority by the Dragon (Satan), the power that was behind the growth of this new beast to try to undo the finished work of Christ upon the Cross.

In 476 AD, the Western Empire under the Caesars fell and broke up into ten regions, as foretold in John's vision, and fulfilled the role of the king "who was to come and then continue a short space". Revelation 13:3 describes this event when it states:

"And I saw one of his heads as it were wounded to death, and his deadly wound was healed; and all the world wondered after the beast."

The fall of the Western Empire would indeed have been a mortal wound to the beast had it not been for the Bishop of Rome filling the power vacuum left by the Caesars. After the breakup of the empire, the nations that had recently converted to Christianity sought the recognition of the Roman Pontiff, as Head of the Church, and gave him spiritual authority over their realms in exchange for secular power. The souls of these nations were given over to the Man of Sin, and these kings would fight on his behalf to destroy those who opposed the edicts of the Synagogue of Satan.

"And the ten horns which you saw are ten kings, which have received no kingdom as yet, but receive power as kings one hour with the beast."

(Revelation 17:12)

The bishops had healed the deadly wound, and the beast was now given a mouth speaking great things and blasphemies, and it was given unto him to make war with the Saints and to overcome them.

Revelation 17:5 describes the Church of Rome as "Mystery, Babylon the Great, the Mother of Harlots and Abominations of the Earth". And here we have the missing piece of the puzzle! Pagan Rome was the controlling power (or king) in Paul's day; before this, we had five kings that were fallen, which, as we have seen, represented Greece and Medo-Persia, leaving Babylon unaccounted for.

Babylon was the first world kingdom influenced by Satan to be in opposition to God, and it created a system of worship that gave honour to the beast. Babylon appeared to fall, but its Pagan practices survived and were carried on in one form or another by the kingdoms that followed. When Emperor Phocas made Boniface III the last Bishop and first Pope of Rome in 607AD,[1] all of these practices were resurrected but disguised as Christian worship. The leaven of false doctrine that was introduced into the Church via the councils of Constantine spread throughout the whole of Christendom under the tyrannical reign of the Papacy.

The beast that was (Babylon) and is not (Babylon appeared to fall) even he is the eighth (the Papacy) and is of the seven (the Papacy is the Little Horn that rises out of the Roman, seventh, head) and goes into perdition (the Papal Antichrist will be destroyed upon Christ's return). Paul prophesied about this event in 2 Thessalonians when he stated that:

"The mystery of iniquity does already work; only he who now restrains [the Caesars] will do so until he be taken out of the way.

And then shall that Wicked be revealed, whom the Lord shall consume with the spirit of his mouth and shall destroy with the brightness of his coming." (2:7–8)

Daniel also foretold this precisely in his seventh chapter, when he described a Little Horn coming up amongst the ten horns on the head of the fourth world kingdom (or beast). This new power would go on to speak great things against the Most High and make war with the Saints and prevail against them until Christ's return.

Satan's offer – which was rejected by Christ – to have power over all the kingdoms of the Earth was willingly accepted by this new power that would become Satan's ambassador on Earth. This man became the head of the false church, the Synagogue of Satan that would cause the world to worship the beast through false doctrine; that is, the Paganism of Babylon disguised as Christianity. We know this man today as the Antichrist, the Pope of Rome.

THE 7 KINGS OF REVELATION XVII

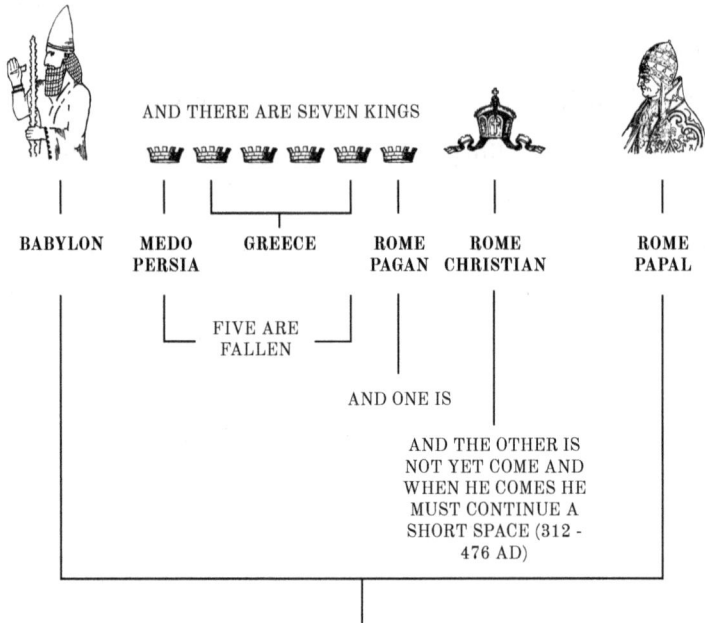

AND THERE ARE SEVEN KINGS

BABYLON   MEDO   GREECE   ROME   ROME   ROME
             PERSIA   PAGAN   CHRISTIAN   PAPAL

FIVE ARE
FALLEN

AND ONE IS

AND THE OTHER IS
NOT YET COME AND
WHEN HE COMES HE
MUST CONTINUE A
SHORT SPACE (312 -
476 AD)

AND THE BEAST THAT WAS, AND IS NOT (SPIRITUAL
BABYLON) EVEN HE IS THE EIGHTH, AND IS OF THE
SEVEN AND GOES INTO PERDITION.

"Babylon was the first world kingdom influenced by Satan to be in opposition to God, and it created a system of worship that gave honour to the beast. Babylon appeared to fall, but its Pagan practices survived and were carried on in one form or another by the kingdoms that followed. When Emperor Phocas made Boniface III the last Bishop and first Pope of Rome in 607AD,[1] all of these practices were resurrected but disguised as Christian worship. The leaven of false doctrine that was introduced into the Church via the councils of Constantine spread throughout the whole of Christendom under the tyrannical reign of the Papacy."

1   Guinness, Henry G., *Romanism and the Reformation from the standpoint of Prophecy*, p.18. A. C. Armstrong & Son, New York. 1887.

CHAPTER VIII

THE TWO WITNESSES AND THE WOMAN
IN THE WILDERNESS

The two witnesses of Revelation chapter 11 are the subject of endless debate. Many people think that they are two literal people, such as Enoch and Elijah, whilst others believe they refer to the Old and New Testaments.

The book of Revelation uses a great deal of symbolic language as John watches a vision of the end times unfold that was sent and signified to him by the angel. The angel tells John:

"'And I will give *power* unto my two witnesses, and they shall prophesy a thousand two hundred *and* threescore days, clothed in sackcloth.

These are the two olive trees and the two candlesticks standing before the God of the earth.'"

(Revelation 11:3–4)

To gain an understanding of who these two witnesses are, we need to let Scripture interpret Scripture. The witnesses are symbolically described as two olive trees and two candlesticks, standing before (in the way of) the God of the Earth

(Satan). In a vision, the Prophet Zechariah saw a golden candlestick standing between two olive trees, and he questioned the angel he talked with as to what they were. The two olive branches were feeding golden oil to the candlestick, and the angel told Zechariah that they were "the two anointed ones that stand by the Lord of the whole earth" (Zechariah 4:11–14). (A prophecy of Jesus and his two witnesses.)

Romans 11 goes into more detail when it describes the Jews, God's chosen people, as being the natural olive tree, and the Gentiles as a wild olive tree. Paul explains that some of the natural branches were broken off through unbelief after rejecting their Messiah; this enabled Gentile believers in Christ to be grafted into the good olive tree through faith.

Revelation 1:20 informs us that candlesticks represent churches, so we can see that the two witnesses are the Jews and Gentiles who make up the true Church, which testifies (or gives witness) that Jesus is the Messiah, the Son of God, and holds to the uncorrupted doctrines of Christ as taught by the Apostles. The fruit of these olive trees produces pure oil, symbolising the faith of the two witnesses, which, in turn, feeds the candlesticks, allowing the light of the gospel to shine brightly.

The prophesying of the two witnesses for a thousand two hundred and three score days (1260 years), clothed in sackcloth, mirrors Revelation 12:6 and 14, where the Woman, who is also symbolic of the Church, flees into the wilderness where God has prepared a place for her to be nourished for the same 1260-year period, from the face of the serpent (Satan).

After Steven was stoned to death in 33AD (the event that marked the end of Daniel's 70th week), we are told that:

"[...] there was a great persecution against the church which was at Jerusalem; and they were all scattered abroad throughout the regions of Judea and Samaria, except the apostles.

And devout men carried Steven *to his burial* and made great lamentation over him.

As for Saul, he made havoc of the church, entering into every house, and hauling off men and women, committing *them* to prison.

Therefore they that were scattered abroad went everywhere preaching the word."

(Acts 8:1–4)

The gospel now went out to the Gentiles, and the true Church started to grow, but often in hiding and isolation to escape the constant threat of persecution. The prophesying of the two witnesses and the Woman in the wilderness are both speaking of the same event that lasted for 1260 years.

(There is a second 1260-year period that the Bible speaks of that is linked to, but comes after, this time, and that is the reign of the Antichrist that was covered in Chapter IV. See the diagram at the end of that chapter.)

Christ's two witnesses testify of Him and stand before Satan, the God of this world, to preach the true gospel – symbolised by fire proceeding out of their mouths to devour their enemies and overcome them with truth.

"'*Is* not my word like as a fire?' says the LORD; 'and like a hammer *that* breaks the rock in pieces?'"

(Jeremiah 23:29)

Whilst the true gospel of Christ was being spread, Satan's influence was already at work, with the false church rising to prominence under the bishops of Rome who would later become the Popes following the decree of Emperor Phocas in 607AD. The Papacy, the office of Satan's ambassador on Earth, came to full power under Gregory VII (Hildebrand) in 1073AD, and just over 100 years later, the full-scale slaughter of the Saints began under Innocent III. The prophesying of the two witnesses and the time of God's protection for the Woman in the wilderness was coming to an end.

"And when they shall have finished their testimony, the beast that ascends out of the bottomless pit shall make war against them, and shall overcome them, and kill them."

(Revelation 11:7)

Revelation 12:17 repeats this story, but the two witnesses are now referred to as the Woman in the wilderness:

"And the Dragon was wroth with the woman, and went to make war with the remnant of her seed, which keep the commandments of God and have the testimony of Jesus Christ."

The Dragon, or the beast from the bottomless pit, refers to Satan, who works through the Papacy to destroy all those who hold fast to the true gospel, as taught by the Apostles, and refuse to bow the knee to Satan's anointed one, the Pope of Rome.

The Waldenses (or Vaudois) of the Piedmont Valley in northern Italy and the Albigenses of southern France are the two groups that are most often associated with Christ's two witnesses in the wilderness. These true followers of Christ suffered unimaginable horrors and genocide for 500 years, beginning in the 12th century, as the Dragon's wrath was poured out upon them without measure by order of the Papal

Antichrist. The full power of the Inquisition, together with the armies who were doing Rome's bidding, was unleashed upon the Saints of the Most High; they spared neither woman nor child as Papal absolution had given them free reign to act without conscience, to commit atrocities that only the Devil himself could inspire a man to carry out.

Many millions would die as the Earth entered its final stage before Christ's return, with the Antichrist being given 1260 years to "continue" his reign of terror after reaching the height of his power in 1073AD, under the pontificate of Gregory VII.

In his vision, John is told to:

"Rise, and measure the temple of God, and the altar, and them that worship therein."

(Revelation 11:1)

The temple of God here refers to the believers in Christ, as confirmed by Paul in 1 Corinthians 3:16 where he says, "Know you not that you are the temple of God and the Spirit of God dwells in you?"

John then receives a further instruction:

"But the court, which is without the temple, leave out and measure it not, for it is given unto the Gentiles, and the holy city shall they tread underfoot forty and two months [1260 years]."

(Revelation 11:2)

The Holy City being trodden under foot by the Gentiles for 1260 years cannot be Jerusalem, as the Gentile powers have been doing this from before the time of Christ to this very day; Islam's third holiest site, the Al-Aqsa Mosque, dominates the city as it stands on the ruins of the Jewish Temple.

Now that the temple of God resides within Christ's two witnesses, they symbolically make up the Holy City, and their treading down by the Gentiles (or non-believers) is a reference to the 1260-year reign of the Antichrist and his war against the Saints who refuse to give their allegiance to the beast, thereby avoiding his mark. The war against the true believers in Christ continues to this day, as prophesied by Daniel when he stated:

"I beheld, and the same horn made war with the saints, and prevailed against them,

Until the Ancient of days came, and judgment was given to the saints of the most High, and the time came that the saints possessed the kingdom."

(Daniel 7:21–22)

After the two witnesses are killed, their dead bodies are said to:

"[...] *lie* in the street of the great city, which spiritually is called Sodom and Egypt, where also our Lord was crucified."

(Revelation 11:8)

Jerusalem is the city that comes to mind when we think of the Crucifixion, but it has to be remembered that Jesus was crucified "outside" the city gates, meaning his death occurred in the Roman province of Judea. Spiritually speaking, Rome can also be described as Sodom and Egypt due to the extremely sinful and idolatrous behaviour of its inhabitants that were no different from the Pagan practices of the past.

The killing of the two witnesses, or the perceived defeat of the true gospel at the hands of the Antichrist-controlled false church, is seen by most commentators as happening just before the start of the Protestant Reformation, or during the French Revolution. It is stated that the Papacy declared all opposition to the supremacy of the Roman Church to be defeated during the Lateran Council of May 1514, exactly three and a half years before Martin Luther posted up his ninety-five theses at Wittenberg. It is also stated that the Bible was banned during the French Revolution, only for the decision to be reversed three and a half years later. Both of these stories sound very plausible and seem to fit with the witnesses appearing to be dead only to have the spirit of life from God enter into them, and then to stand upon their feet before their enemies (Revelation 11:11). It's very easy to attribute stories like these to the fulfilment of prophecy, but a close reading of the chapter shows that the event is still in the future, with the timeline ruling them both out – no matter how well they appear to fit.

The killing of the two witnesses occurs just before the sounding of the seventh trumpet, when the second woe is over, and the third comes quickly (Revelation 11:14–15). Here lies our problem: none of the trumpets are even given to the seven angels until the seventh seal is opened, and as of 2021 (the time of writing), it is clear from the description of the seals that both the sixth and seventh seals remain unopened!

When the fifth seal is opened, John sees the souls of them that were slain for the word of God and for the testimony which they held. This was a vision of the martyrs of Christ who died during the time of great slaughter and Papal persecutions. The Saints are symbolically seen "crying out" to God, asking Him how long it will be before He judges and avenges their blood.

"[...] and it was said unto them, that they should rest yet for a little season, until their fellow servants also, and their brethren, that should be killed as they *were*."

(Revelation 6:11)

This is the time we are living in now, in which we have endured two World Wars, and many other persecutions, all orchestrated by the Papacy to further its goal of world domination.

The events from verse eight of Revelation 11 are all in the future, so we can only speculate as to their precise meaning; although, it's clear from the language used and the timeline that the raising of the two witnesses and their ascension up to heaven in a cloud is the same event described in the Olivet Discourse, when Christ returns to gather his elect. Matthew 24, Mark 13 and Luke 21 all describe this event as happening after the time of great tribulation and great signs being seen in the heavens – a reference to the opening of the sixth seal, "where the sun became black as sackcloth of hair, and the moon became as blood" (Revelation 6:12). The Prophet Daniel also foresaw this "time of trouble, such as never was since there was a nation," and the first resurrection of the Saints (Daniel 12:1–2).

Revelation 11 ends with the raising of the two witnesses of Christ and the sounding of the seventh and final trumpet. A second witness that this is the event being talked about in the Olivet Discourse can be found in Paul's first letter to the Corinthians, where he states:

"Behold, I show you a mystery: We shall not all sleep, but we shall all be changed,

In a moment, in the twinkling of an eye, at the last trump; for the trumpet shall sound, and the dead shall be raised incorruptible, and we shall be changed."

CHAPTER IX

THE CRUCIFIXION CONTRADICTION?

On the surface, the day and year of the Crucifixion may not seem that important, but if the adversary saw value in hiding it, then it is our duty to uncover the truth.

Matthew's 12th chapter records that Jesus answered certain of the scribes and Pharisees, who were seeking after a sign, by telling them that He would be three days and three nights in the heart of the earth, just as Jonah had been in the belly of the whale. It is universally taught, in the organised church, that Jesus died on the Cross on a Friday afternoon with His Resurrection occurring on Sunday morning – and here lies our problem. It is impossible to get even part of three days and three nights between these two times. Many people have noticed this, but it is just ignored as Church tradition dictates that Christians should celebrate Good Friday and Easter Sunday.

From the very beginning, it has been Satan's goal to sow doubt in our minds. It all started when he deceived Eve into eating fruit from the tree in the midst of the garden that God had warned would bring death – "You shall not surely die," hissed the Serpent! The Church of Rome has influenced and dictated doctrine for over 1500 years, teaching that when we are faced with an apparent mystery that doesn't seem to make sense, we shouldn't concern ourselves with such things but, instead, we should just put our faith in the church. However, when our faith is tested, which happens to most of us at some point in our lives, contradictions (such as Friday afternoon to Sunday morning equalling three days and three nights) can plant a seed of doubt that may lead you to question the validity of Scripture, and ultimately destroy your faith.

This chapter will show that there is no such contradiction in the Crucifixion story and that the problem, as always, lies within man's false interpretation of Scripture. When the gospels are studied closely, there are many clues that, when pieced together, all point to only one possible day that precisely matches the narrative in every detail.

First, we will look at the year of Christ's Crucifixion and show how Jesus's own words combine with known history to identify it. Many arguments are put forward for the year that Jesus died, nearly all of them between 27 and 33 AD, with 33 AD being the most popular. Although the year of the Crucifixion is the subject of much debate, there is unanimous agreement on the date of another event around this time that is incredibly helpful to us. The destruction of Jerusalem and its temple during Passover of 70 AD appears to be a fixed point in history that we can use to identify the year in question.

God knows the end from the beginning, so you can be certain that everything prophesied will happen exactly as foretold and precisely on time. The Crucifixion is a perfect example of this, and the gospels contain a prophecy that has been overlooked by almost everyone, a prophecy that points to the year of Christ's death.

Matthew and Luke both recount how Jesus spoke to the people, scribes and Pharisees after they had asked to see a sign from him:

"[Jesus] answered and said unto them, 'An evil and adulterous generation seeks after a sign; and there shall no sign be given to it, but the sign of the Prophet Jonah.

'For as Jonah was three days and three nights in the whale's belly, so shall the Son of man be three days and three nights in the heart of the earth.'"

(Matthew 12:39–42)

Luke puts it slightly differently when he states:

"For as Jonah was a sign unto the Ninevites, so shall also the Son of man be to this generation."

(Luke 11:30)

Most people look at these verses and take the sign of Jonah to represent Christ being dead for three days and three nights prior to His Resurrection, but there is a much deeper meaning, which is expanded upon in the following verses and relates to the men of Nineveh.

Both gospels are almost identical when they state:

"The men of Nineveh shall rise in judgment with this generation and shall condemn it, because they repented at the preaching of Jonah; and behold, a greater than Jonah is here."

So why does Jesus go into detail about the men of Nineveh if the point he was making only related to the length of time he would be dead being equal to the time Jonah spent in the great fish? The fact is, Jesus was giving the Jews the same prophetic warning that Jonah had given to the people of Nineveh. God sent Jonah to the people of Nineveh to warn them that, unless they repented and turned to God, their city would be destroyed in forty days. Much to Jonah's surprise, instead of killing him for giving this warning, the people did repent, and their city was saved.

When Jesus came near to Jerusalem:

"[...] he beheld the city, and wept over it,

saying, 'If you had known, even you, at least in this your day, the things *which belong* unto your peace! But now they are hid from your eyes.

For the days shall come upon you that your enemies shall cast a trench about you and compass you round, and keep you in on every side,

and shall lay you even with the ground, and your children within you; and they shall not leave in you one stone upon another, because you knew not the time of your visitation."

(Luke 19:41–44)

As we have seen previously in the prophecies of Daniel, a day is prophetically counted as a year, and Numbers 14:34 is a perfect example of this:

"'After the number of the days in which you searched the land, even forty days, each day for a year, shall you bear your iniquities, even forty years, and you shall know My breach of promise.'"

Jesus was warning the people of Jerusalem that, unless they repented and accepted Him as their Messiah, their city would be destroyed in 40 years. The men of Nineveh had heeded this same warning when a lesser man than Jesus had come to them, but the Jews failed to accept their Messiah and suffered the consequences at the appointed time. For this reason, the men of Nineveh would be justified in condemning that generation at the judgement, because the Jews failed to listen to a much greater Prophet than the one that had been sent to them!

We have already seen how Jerusalem was destroyed during Passover of 70AD, so if Jesus was crucified during Passover of 30AD then this would be the perfect fulfilment of the prophetic warning that Jesus gave to the Jews, and the sign of Jonah.

A second witness for the year of Christ's Crucifixion can be found in Daniel 9:25, which states:

"Know therefore and understand,

That from the going forth of the commandment

To restore and to build Jerusalem

Unto the Messiah the Prince

Shall be seven weeks, and threescore and two weeks."

According to scholars, the decree to rebuild Jerusalem was given by Artaxerxes in either 457BC or 458BC, with 458BC being a perfect prophetic match for Christ's ministry and death.

This was a prophecy, so the weeks are periods of seven years; add seven weeks to threescore and two weeks, and we come to sixty-nine weeks of years, or 483 years. When we count forward 483 years from 458BC, we arrive at 26AD – for the year that Jesus started His ministry – when He was about thirty years old.

Daniel 9:27 tells us that he would:

"[...] confirm the covenant with many for one week;

And in the midst of the week he shall cause the sacrifice and the oblation to cease."

This is a reference to the 70th and final week of Daniel's prophecy, which relates to Jesus's suffering on the Cross being the final sacrifice acceptable to God. The Crucifixion occurred in the midst of the 70th week of years; in other words, three and a half years into His ministry, during Passover of 30AD. This caused the sacrificial system to end in God's eyes as Jesus stated with His last words before giving up the spirit, "It is finished."

The gospel would continue to be preached to the Jews for a further three and a half years after the Crucifixion, as God kept His promise to give them a full 70 weeks (or 490 years) to repent and turn to Him. They failed, and Daniel 9:27 ends by telling us the consequences of their failure to end the transgression when it states:

"And for the overspreading of abominations [the continuation of sacrifices] he shall make it desolate,

Even until the consummation, and that determined,

Shall be poured upon the desolate."

With this in mind, it's safe to say that all evidence, both prophetic and historical, points to 30AD as the year that Christ was crucified.

We now turn our attention to the date. Scripture is very clear that these events happened around the time of Passover, with the book of Exodus telling us that Passover occurs during the first month of the year, the month of Abib. After the Babylonian exile, the months were renamed, with Abib becoming Nisan; this first month of the Jewish calendar begins around what we call late March.

The month is certain, but the actual day is the subject of a great deal of confusion because the gospels appear to imply that Jesus ate the Passover meal with His disciples and also that He was crucified before the Passover; so how is this to be understood?

The 14th day of the first month is often referred to as the Passover, or the preparation day for the Passover, which is a more accurate description. This is the day when all leaven is to be removed from the home and, during the Exodus, it was the day when a lamb without blemish was sacrificed and its blood painted on the lintel and upright door posts so that when the LORD passed through the land of Egypt, He would spare the firstborn in all homes marked with the blood of the lamb. This event foreshadowed the fact that Christians would have death "pass over" them when they put their faith in the shed blood of Christ upon the upright and horizontal beams of the Cross, the sacrifice that paid the price for the sins of all who would believe.

The method of reckoning time that was observed in Jesus's day, was very different from what we are used to now, and this only adds to the confusion. Instead of the new day starting immediately after midnight, it would start at sunset or approximately 7 p.m., so when we read that the Passover lamb was sacrificed on the 14th day at evening, this could mean the evening that starts that day or the evening that ends it! Obviously, this is a problem if we are trying to pinpoint a precise time, but a careful study of the Exodus story gives us our answer.

The order of events is very clear. Firstly, the lamb would be killed on the 14th day and its blood painted on the door frame of the home to be protected. The lamb would then be cooked and eaten that evening, with God passing over the land of Egypt around midnight to kill the firstborn of all who were not protected by its blood. In the early hours of the 15th day, the children of Israel were ejected from Egypt by Pharaoh, the event we know as the Exodus. The Passover lamb could not have been killed on the evening that starts the 14th day because the following morning would still be the 14th and Scripture is clear that the Exodus, which was the first full day of unleavened bread, started on the 15th day of the first month.

The Synoptic gospels of Matthew, Mark and Luke all state that the first day of unleavened bread was when the Passover was to be killed. This appears to be a contradiction as the seven-day feast of unleavened bread is between the 15th day and the 21st, with the lamb being killed on the 14th day, the preparation for the Passover (Numbers 28:16–17). The gospel of John asserts that Jesus was crucified on the preparation day, the 14th (19:14–18). So, who is correct? As we have seen throughout this book, the Bible is the inspired word of God, and apparent contradictions disappear when deeper study is undertaken.

1 Corinthians 5:7 tells us that "Christ our Passover is sacrificed for us". When John the Baptist saw Jesus coming unto him, he said "Behold the Lamb of God, which takes away the sin of the world" (John 1:29).

If Jesus was to fulfil this prophecy, then he had to die at the time appointed for the Passover lamb to be killed, the 14th day of the first month, as the sun was going down (Exodus 12:6 & Deuteronomy 16:6). The clue to this apparent problem can be found in Exodus 12:18, which states:

"In the first *month*, on the fourteenth day of the month at even, you shall eat unleavened bread until the twenty-first day of the month at even."

This implies that the Passover meal started before the 14th day had ended and continued through the night, which was the beginning of the 15th or first full day of unleavened bread.

"You shall not offer the blood of my sacrifice with leaven; neither shall the sacrifice of the feast of the passover be left unto the morning."

(Exodus 34:25)

Counting from the end of the 14th to the end of the 21st day, we have seven full days, the 15th to the 21st. Because the Passover meal straddled the 14th and 15th days, the synoptic gospels were correct when they stated that the Passover was killed on the first day of unleavened bread, and John accurately described the Crucifixion as occurring on the preparation day!

Further confusion arises from the fact that the synoptic gospels all speak of the disciples coming to Jesus and asking Him where they should go to prepare for Him to eat the Passover, which is followed by a description of the meal Jesus ate with them. If Jesus died on the day of preparation for the Passover, then how could he have eaten the Passover meal? All four gospels are in agreement that Jesus was crucified on the preparation day (Matthew 27:62, Mark 15:42 and Luke 23:54), and John 19:14 gives us extra details that help us to understand this apparent problem.

On the morning that followed Jesus's arrest in the garden, *after* He had eaten with His disciples, John 18:28 states:

"Then led they Jesus from Caiaphas unto the Hall of Judgment, and it was early. And they themselves went not into the Judgment Hall, lest they should be defiled, but that they might eat the Passover."

We have seen that the Passover meal is eaten at evening; this event was taking place in the early hours of the morning, and the Passover would not occur until that coming evening at the end of the day. This means that the meal Jesus ate with His disciples was at the very beginning of the day of preparation, rather than at the end of it when the official Passover meal was to be eaten. Only two options are left open to us: either Jesus had an early Passover meal or He only hoped to share Passover with His disciples, and the meal He did share with them was just a supper. Again, John gives us a further clue when he states:

"Now before the feast of the passover, when Jesus knew that his hour was come that he should depart out of this world unto the Father, having loved his own which were in the world, he loved them unto the end.

And supper being ended, the devil having now put into the heart of Judas Iscariot, Simon's *son*, to betray him."

(John 13:1–2)

These verses show that Jesus was eating a "supper" that was "before" the feast of the Passover. Another clue is given a few verses later when Jesus is telling His disciples that one of them would betray Him and that it would be the one He would give a piece of bread to after He had dipped it. After He gave the bread to Judas Iscariot, John states:

"And after the piece of bread, Satan entered into him. Then said Jesus unto him, 'That you do, do quickly.'

Now no man at the table knew for what intent he spoke this unto him.

For some *of them* thought, because Judas had the bag, that Jesus had said unto him, 'Buy *those things* that we have need of against the feast.'"

(John 13:27–29)

We saw in verse 1 that this meal was before the Passover, in verse 2 that the supper had ended, and in verse 29 that the disciples thought Judas was going to buy things for the feast. Obviously, he wouldn't have been going to buy things for the meal, identified as a supper, that had already ended, but rather for the feast of the Passover the following evening, the one Jesus desired to eat with His disciples but knew He never would.

As stated at the beginning of this chapter, tradition holds that Jesus was crucified on Friday and was resurrected early on Sunday morning, before sunrise. This not only goes against prophecy, but also contradicts Jesus's own words when He stated:

"'For as Jonah was three days and three nights in the whale's belly; so shall the Son of man be three days and three nights in the heart of the earth.'"

(Matthew 12:40)

If we count Friday as the first day, this would be followed by Saturday night, as the Jewish day follows the Genesis account by starting with the night: "And God called the light Day, and the darkness He called Night. And the evening and the morning were the first day" (Genesis 1:5). Saturday day would be the second day, which would be followed by Sunday night, the second night. Matthew 28:1 and John

20:1 both state that Mary Magdalene came to the sepulchre early on the first day of the week before dawn and found the tomb empty, meaning that Sunday night was the last period of time that Jesus spent in the grave. Even when we count Friday as the first day, we only have a maximum of two days and two nights, making a Friday Crucifixion impossible.

The Friday Crucifixion is only backed up by a simplified reading of Mark 15:42 and Luke 23:54, which both tell how Joseph of Arimathea went to Pontius Pilate to ask for the body of Jesus because it was the preparation day and the Sabbath was drawing near. The Sabbath mentioned here is taken to mean the weekly Saturday Sabbath, despite the fact that the day following the preparation day for the Passover is always a High Sabbath, the first full day of unleavened bread, no matter which day of the week it falls upon. John's gospel confirms this when he states:

"The Jews, therefore, because it was the preparation, that the bodies should not remain upon the cross on the Sabbath day (for that Sabbath day was a high day), besought Pilate that their legs might be broken, and *that* they might be taken away."

(John 19:31)

If we rule out Friday, then what about Wednesday, which seems to be the most popular alternative for the Crucifixion? Wednesday allows for a full seventy-two hours (or three full days and three full nights) for Christ to be in the grave, and for a couple of years, I also believed that this was the day. However, in order for Wednesday to be the day of the Crucifixion, the four hours or so of that day that Christ was dead would not be included in the count, nor any part of Sunday, which is a big problem.

Matthew 27:51 informs us that when Jesus died:

"The veil of the temple was torn in two from the top to the bottom; and the earth did quake, and the rocks were split."

In the following chapter, he tells us that:

"At the end of Sabbath, as it began to dawn toward the first *day* of the week [Sunday] came Mary Magdalene and the other Mary to see the sepulchre.

And behold, there was a great earthquake; for the angel of the LORD descended from heaven and came and rolled back the stone from the door, and sat upon it."

(Matthew 28:1–2)

Jesus's death was marked with a great earthquake, so it makes perfect sense that His Resurrection was marked in the same way. A Wednesday Crucifixion would necessitate the Resurrection at the end of Saturday, but it makes no sense for Christ's Resurrection to be marked with silence, only to have a great earthquake the following morning when the angel rolled back the stone on the tomb that was already empty, and had been for at least ten hours!

Further evidence that Jesus was resurrected on Sunday and not Saturday comes from the fact that He is referred to on many occasions in Scripture as the "first fruits".

"But now is Christ risen from the dead, *and* become the first fruits of them that slept."

(1 Corinthians 15:20)

We have already seen how Jesus's death was the perfect fulfilment of the feast of the Passover, and His Resurrection was the fulfilment of the Feast of the First Fruits, too. This feast always takes place on the day that follows the weekly Sabbath during the seven-day feast of unleavened bread, in other words, on Sunday, the first day of the week (Leviticus 23:10–11, 15–17).

The other problem with a Wednesday Crucifixion is something that always bothered me deeply and forced me to reevaluate what I had previously thought. If Jesus died on Wednesday, the following day (Thursday) would have been a High Sabbath day, the first full day of unleavened bread where no work could be done. The next day (Friday) would have been the preparation day for the weekly Sabbath, where work could be done. This would have been followed by Saturday, the weekly Sabbath, where no work could be done; and the following morning, before dawn (Sunday), the women went to the sepulchre to anoint Jesus's body. We know that no work could be done on the day following the Crucifixion due to it being a High Sabbath, but if Christ was crucified on Wednesday, then His body could have been anointed by the women on the Friday, when work could take place. Obviously, this would have involved sharing the duties of preparing for the Saturday Sabbath amongst the other women, but the alternative would have involved willingly leaving Jesus in the tomb to decompose for a further two full days, which is inconceivable! There is no getting around this problem, and it just adds to the weight of evidence that rules Wednesday out for the day of Christ's death.

Thursday is a day that is hardly ever mentioned in relation to the Crucifixion, and for good reason; Satan is more than happy to have people arguing over two incorrect days because both suit his purposes and allow the truth to go unnoticed in the background. As we shall see, only Thursday matches Scripture in every detail, without any contradiction, and gives us the final piece to the puzzle.

Friday just doesn't give us enough days; Wednesday gives us too many and makes no sense when we see that it involves leaving Christ's body to decompose longer than necessary; but neither of these problems exist with Thursday. If Jesus died on Thursday, the following day would have been a High Sabbath, so the women couldn't anoint his body; the next day would have been the weekly Sabbath; so, the first possible opportunity for them to go to the tomb would have been on Sunday, the first day of the week, which is what Scripture describes.

Another clear conformation for Thursday comes from Luke, where his gospel speaks of the events that occurred on the day of Christ's Resurrection. We have established how this was on Sunday:

"And behold, two of them went that same day to a village called Emmaus, which was from Jerusalem *about* threescore furlongs."

(Luke 24:13)

During this journey, whilst they were discussing the things that had happened, Jesus Himself joined with them, asking what they were talking about and why they were sad, but they didn't recognise him.

"And one of them, whose name was Cleopas, answering, said unto him, 'Are you only a stranger in Jerusalem, and have not known the things which are come to pass there in these days?'

And he said unto them, 'What things?' And they said unto him, 'Concerning Jesus of Nazareth, which was a prophet mighty in deed and word before God and all the people,

'And how the chief priests and our rulers delivered him to be condemned to death, and have crucified him.

THE CRUCIFIXION CONTRADICTION?

'But we trusted that it had been he which should have redeemed Israel; and beside all this, today is the third day since these things were done.'"

(Luke 24:18–21)

There is no doubt that the meeting on the road to Emmaus occurred on Sunday, so if Sunday was the third day "since these things were done", then Saturday would be the second day "since" and Friday the first day "since", which would make Thursday the day when they were done.

Another huge confirmation for Thursday, which also seems to have gone unnoticed, comes from John's gospel, where he states:

"Then Jesus, six days before the passover, came to Bethany."

"On the next day, much people that were come to the feast, when they heard that Jesus was coming to Jerusalem,

took branches of palm trees, and went forth to meet him, and cried:

'Hosanna!

'Blessed *is* the King of Israel

that comes in the name of the LORD!'"

(John 12:1, 12–13)

The Passover starts at the end of the 14th day, the evening that is also the beginning of the 15th day. We have already seen how God passed over the land of Egypt at around midnight on the 15th, with the Exodus occurring a few hours later, leading into the dawn of that same day. With this in mind, one day before the Passover would have been Thursday 14th Abib, the preparation day for the Passover. Two days before would have been Wednesday 13th, three days before would have been Tuesday 12th, four days before would have been Monday 11th, five days before would have been Sunday 10th, which leaves Saturday 9th as six days before, when Jesus arrived in Bethany.

We see from John's 12th chapter that Jesus had supper with Martha and Lazarus, her brother whom he had raised from the dead, and it was at this supper that Mary anointed him with very expensive ointment. If Jesus had arrived on Friday, then this would have been the weekly Sabbath meal and not just a supper; if he had arrived on Sunday, then this would cause major problems as it would lead to a Friday Crucifixion, which has been ruled out for many reasons.

With Jesus arriving in Bethany on Saturday 9th Abib, the next day, when he entered Jerusalem, would have been Sunday 10th, or Palm Sunday as it is known today. Exodus 12:3 tells us that the 10th day of the first month is when the Passover lamb was to be chosen; Jesus's Triumphal entry into Jerusalem, where He was acknowledged by the crowd as the King of Israel, was the perfect fulfilment of this prophetic command. Exodus goes on to tell us that the lamb was to be kept until the 14th day of the same month before it was to be killed by the whole assembly of the congregation of Israel. If Sunday was the 10th, Monday would be the 11th, Tuesday the 12th and Wednesday the 13th, which means that Thursday would have been the 14th day of the month of Abib in the year 30AD, the preparation day for the Passover, which was perfectly fulfilled by Jesus Christ, the Lamb of God who takes away the sins of the world.

When Jesus spoke His final words, "It is finished", He knew that His death would fulfil all those things written about Him in the Law and the Prophets. Christ's sinless life of obedience defeated the work of the serpent (to subvert God's plan when Adam brought sin and death into the world through disobedience to God). Christ fulfilled God's promise to Abraham that He would provide the sacrificial lamb. Gabriel's prophetic message to Daniel that Messiah would come at the beginning of the 69th week of years was fulfilled, as was the fact that His death in the midst of that week would cause the sacrifice and oblation to cease. Jonah's prophetic warning to the Ninevites was realised in Christ as the Jews failed to heed the same warning that Jesus extended to them, bringing about the destruction of their city forty years later; 2300 years of desolation was determined upon them when they failed to end the transgression by anointing their Messiah at the end of Daniel's 70th week, the event that allowed the Gentiles to be grafted into spiritual Israel through faith in the one whom the Jews had rejected.

Christ's finished work upon the Cross brought about a new and better covenant that allows for all – both Jew and Gentile – to enter the Kingdom and gain eternal life. God has extended a free gift by grace to us all, that through faith in His Son and what He achieved on our behalf, we too can receive adoption as Children of God. We are all given the ability to recognise this incredible opportunity that should be grasped with both hands. Failure to take advantage of this free gift may result in wailing and gnashing of teeth when the terrible reality of its rejection dawns on those who turned their backs on Jesus and refused to open the door when he stood there patiently knocking, waiting to be let into their life!

THE CRUCIFIXION

THURSDAY 14TH ABIB 30AD

(JOHN 12:1)

SATURDAY 9TH ABIB	EVE				
	DAY		JESUS ARRIVES IN BETHANY		6 DAYS BEFORE PASSOVER
SUNDAY 10TH ABIB	EVE		HAS SUPPER WITH MARTHA AND LAZARUS		
	DAY		JESUS ARRIVES IN JERUSALEM. THE LAMB IS CHOSEN (EXODUS 12:3)		5 DAYS BEFORE PASSOVER
MONDAY 11TH ABIB	EVE				
	DAY				4 DAYS BEFORE PASSOVER
TUESDAY 12TH ABIB	EVE				
	DAY				3 DAYS BEFORE PASSOVER
WEDNESDAY 13TH ABIB	EVE				
	DAY				2 DAYS BEFORE PASSOVER
THURSDAY 14TH ABIB	EVE	THE LAST SUPPER	JESUS ARRESTED AND SENTENCED		
	DAY	PREPARATION DAY	(EXODUS 12:6) JESUS CRUCIFIED JESUS BURIED	1ST DAY	1 DAY BEFORE PASSOVER
FRIDAY 15TH ABIB	EVE	THE PASSOVER		1ST NIGHT	
	DAY	HIGH SABBATH		2ND DAY	1 DAY SINCE THESE THINGS HAPPENED
SATURDAY 16TH ABIB	EVE	WEEKLY SABBATH		2ND NIGHT	
	DAY			3RD DAY	2 DAYS SINCE THESE THINGS HAPPENED
SUNDAY 17TH ABIB	EVE			3RD NIGHT	
	DAY	FIRST FRUITS	JESUS RISEN TALKS TO MEN ON ROAD TO EMMAUS		3 DAYS SINCE THESE THINGS HAPPENED

(LUKE 24:18-21)

CHAPTER X

THE SABBATH QUESTION

This chapter is a late addition to a book that I thought was finished. It serves to show how we never stop learning and should always be willing to test long-held beliefs, to prove all things and hold fast that which is good.

The subject is a very contentious one that has divided Christians for centuries; recently, I brought it up during a study with friends and I may have lost one of them as a result. The fact that merely addressing this subject, to see if we may have been deceived, brought about such a strong reaction, made me realise how important it was to do a much deeper study, to see if Scripture agrees with tradition.

The Fourth Commandment states "Remember the Sabbath day, to keep it Holy." Early in the 4th century, Emperor Constantine enacted that on "the venerable day of the sun", the law courts and all workshops should be closed, and the urban population should rest.[1] This legal transfer of the obligations set out in the Fourth Commandment from Saturday, the seventh day of the week, to Sunday, the first day of the week, became one of the foundational doctrines of the Roman

Catholic Church, which, together with the Trinity, moulded Christianity into an "image to the beast" (Revelation 13:14).

There is no doubt that the Sabbath day was, and always will be, on the seventh day, which is Saturday, and here lies our problem: the vast majority of "organised" Christian churches come together to worship on Sunday, in line with the Church of Rome.

When the Protestant Reformation started in earnest, following the publication of Luther's ninety-five theses in 1517, Protestants continued to worship on Sundays, much to the delight of Rome, who accused them of still following "her authority", as there was no reference in Scripture to the transference of the Sabbath from Saturday to Sunday. On the surface, this seems very clear-cut; either you follow Scripture, which states the seventh day (Saturday), or you follow Rome and abstain from work on Sundays to keep it as a special day of worship. I used to think this way too, as worship on Sunday was clearly a Roman deception and they even admit that it is their "mark" of authority and nothing more.

As we see repeatedly, Satan is extremely subtle, the master of deception, and this appears to be the case here, too. Whilst Christians are arguing over which day they should worship upon, they lose sight of the fact that Sabbath day obligations were never taught by Jesus or expected of Gentiles.

Pleasing God is obviously a good thing, but trying too hard can blind our eyes to the message of Scripture and put us in danger of trying to earn our own salvation, when Christ has already paid that price for us. Many Christians cherry-pick aspects of the law from the Old Covenant, such as abstaining from eating pork, doing no work on the Sabbath and observing one or more of the feast days in their own ways, despite none of this being taught. The New Testament is very clear in its message regarding the law that the Sabbath day obligations belong to:

"Stand fast therefore in the liberty wherewith Christ has made us free, and be not entangled again with the yoke of bondage.

Behold, I, Paul, say unto you that if you be circumcised, Christ shall profit you nothing.

For I testify again to every man that is circumcised that he is a debtor to do the whole law.

Christ is become of no effect unto you, whosoever of you are justified by the law; you are fallen from grace."

(Galatians 5:1–4)

Paul was giving a very clear message to Christians not to fall back into the ways of the Old Covenant by trying to become justified through following the law, which he admits, even their fathers were unable to keep (Acts 15:10). We are now justified by grace, through our faith in the fact that Jesus was the only man to ever live who kept the law perfectly, thus paying the price for the sins of mankind against God. Our faith is what saves us because, by the grace of God, the righteousness of Christ is imputed upon the true believer, so God now sees us *in Him* and we are accepted in His eyes, despite lacking the ability to fulfil the law personally.

When Jesus taught the people about not labouring for food that perishes, but to seek out that food which endures to everlasting life, He spoke of the spiritual food, the word of God that He was speaking and that, if understood and followed, would lead to immortality. Many didn't understand as they still had the mindset of being under the law, so:

"Then said they unto him, 'What shall we do, that we might work the works of God?'

Jesus answered, and said unto them, 'This is the work of God, that you believe on him whom he has sent.'"

(John 6:28–29)

Jesus went to great pains to point out that it was faith that was required, not the blind following of ordinances without understanding the meaning behind them, which is why He often spoke in parables. Rather than giving a list of rules to be followed, Christ wanted His followers to understand the message He was bringing, and to have changed hearts.

The law was a schoolmaster to teach obedience to God's chosen people, Israel, and together with the Prophets, they painted a picture of the coming Messiah that should have been recognised. The Prophet Jeremiah foretold of a New Covenant that would not be according to the covenant that God made with the house of Israel when he brought them out of the land of Egypt. This New Covenant would involve God's people having the law written upon their hearts:

"[...] not with ink, but with the Spirit of the living God, not in tables of stone, but in fleshy tables of the heart."

(2 Corinthians 3:3)

Paul goes on to say that God:

"[...] has made us able ministers of the new testament; not of the letter, but of the spirit; for the letter kills, but the spirit gives life."

(2 Corinthians 3:6)

"Before faith came, we were kept under the law, shut up unto the faith, which should afterwards be revealed.

Wherefore the law was our schoolmaster *to bring us* unto Christ, that we might be justified by faith.

But after that faith is come, we are no longer under a schoolmaster,

For you are all children of God by faith in Christ Jesus."

(Galatians 3:23–26)

The Old Covenant, including the Ten Commandments, has been replaced, but that doesn't mean that the spirit of the law and what it was teaching is gone. Jesus didn't come to destroy the law or the Prophets, but to fulfil them. His message was one of an even higher standard than that of the scribes and Pharisees, who had added more and more restrictions to God's law in an effort to earn salvation through works, rather than by faith. The Jewish leadership were trying to follow the law to the letter and had become obsessed with legalism in much the same way the Taliban have been strictly enforcing Islamic law in recent times. Unfortunately, they lost all sight of the meaning behind God's law, so when their Messiah came, they only recognised the threat to their own authority!

Jesus deliberately provoked them by healing seven times on the Sabbath day in order to demonstrate the hypocrisy of those who were blindly enforcing the law. He gave rest to all those he healed by relieving them of their afflictions, and from the end of Matthew's 11th chapter, we see a picture starting to emerge of the true meaning behind the Sabbath.

"'Come unto me, all you that labour, and are heavy laden, and I will give you rest.

Take my yoke upon you and learn of me, for I am meek and lowly in heart, and you shall find rest unto your souls.

For my yoke is easy and my burden is light."

(Matthew 11:28–30)

Immediately following this statement, chapter 12 begins with Jesus and his disciples travelling through the corn on the Sabbath day, and, being hungry, began to pluck corn to eat. When the Pharisees saw it, they contended with Jesus about His disciples doing that which was unlawful on the Sabbath day. Jesus answered by explaining that Scripture told how David, when hungry, entered into the house of God and ate the shewbread, which was also unlawful. Before he departed into the Synagogue, Jesus left them with a final thought by stating:

"'But I say unto you, that in this place is *one* greater than the temple.

'But if you had known what *this* means, "I will have mercy, and not sacrifice," you would not have condemned the guiltless.

'For the Son of man is Lord even of the Sabbath day.'"

(Matthew 12:6–8)

Jesus was quoting from Hosea chapter 6, which speaks of Israel's transgression of God's covenant, and gives a plea to return to the Lord. Verse 6 says:

"For I desire mercy and not sacrifice; and the knowledge of God more than burnt offerings."

It is no coincidence that the chapter begins with a prophecy of Christ Himself when it states:

"Come, and let us return unto the LORD;

For he has torn, and he will heal us;

he has smitten, and he will bind us up.

After two days will he revive us;

in the third day he will raise us up,

and we shall live in his sight."

(Hosea 6:1–2)

Prophetically speaking, a day can be seen as a thousand years, meaning that we are now very close to the end of the second prophetic day (or 2000th year) since Christ's rejection and Crucifixion in 30AD. During the third prophetic day referred to by Hosea, Christ will return to set up His millennial reign upon the Earth, which will also be the seventh prophetic day of Earth's history, as Jesus appeared after approximately 4000 years had elapsed since Creation.

Jesus's 1000-year millennial reign will be the fulfilment of the seventh day Sabbath rest, when Satan will be bound, and peace, truth and justice will prevail upon Earth. The Christian who now lives by faith can rest from the works of the law, which will not return until Christ's Second Coming. During this time, the Prophets tell how the law will once again go out to the world, to instil obedience in readiness for Satan's release to deceive the nations once more.

Throughout the book of Acts, we see many occasions where Paul would teach on the Sabbath day, which led people to believe that the Apostles kept the Sabbath after the Crucifixion. However, as seen repeatedly, when we look closely at Scripture, we find that it doesn't actually say what we thought it did, with many doctrines having to be read into the text.

Paul, who was well versed in the law, would go to the synagogue on the Sabbath day to reason with, and hopefully persuade, some of the Jews that Jesus was the promised Messiah. There is no evidence that Paul did this because he was keeping the Sabbath, but from the context, it can be seen that it was his best opportunity to speak to the people and reveal the truth of the gospel to them. His efforts were often met with anger and violence because, to many Jews, his teachings against continuing in the Law of Moses were seen as heresy. When Paul came to Antioch, he went into the synagogue on the Sabbath day and, after the reading of the law and the Prophets, was invited to speak. Paul spoke of the history of the Jews and how Jesus was that descendant of King David who God had promised to raise to be a saviour unto Israel.

"For David, after he had served his own generation by the will of God, fell on sleep, and was laid unto his fathers, and saw corruption;

but he, whom God raised again, saw no corruption.

Be it known unto you therefore, men *and* brethren, that through this man is preached unto you the forgiveness of sins;

and by him all that believe are justified from all things, from which you could not be justified by the law of Moses."

(Acts 13:36–39)

After his teachings, many believed, both Jew and Gentile, but the Jewish leadership raised persecution against Paul and Barnabas and expelled them out of the district.

On another occasion, when Paul was in Philippi of Macedonia, he went out of the city on the Sabbath day, by a riverside, to speak to the women whose custom it was to meet for prayer. A woman named Lydia, together with her household, believed the words of Paul and were all baptised. It's clear that Paul wasn't keeping the Sabbath in any legal sense but, instead, was using it as an opportunity to reveal Jesus to those who would come together on that day.

Strictly following the Sabbath today comes from a well-intentioned but misguided notion that God still requires us to follow ordinances that were given to Israel under the Old Covenant. When a new covenant or contract is provided, the old is automatically made obsolete, but far too many people ignore this and revert back to the law, despite the warnings given in Scripture.

It is very important to read and study the whole Bible, both Old and New Testaments, but we have to acknowledge that the Old Testament was preparing the Jewish nation for the coming of the prophesied Messiah. The Old Testament, with its covenant between God and physical Israel, is still vital to Christians today as it gives us the background and foundation of our faith. Christ was the fulfilment of all those things written about Messiah in the law and the Prophets, so we have to pay attention to His new teachings that supersede the ordinances He came to fulfil.

Throughout the New Testament, we see Jesus constantly putting Himself in conflict with the Jewish leadership who were seemingly upholding the law. The hard-hearted attitude that Jesus repeatedly faced persists today, where blind legalism is practised with no understanding of the meaning that these laws were trying to instil. If a literal seventh day Sabbath rest was still required, where no work was to be done, then Jesus and the Apostles would have been very clear to point this out, but they did not. All of the other commandments, apart from the Fourth, are confirmed and expanded upon, but no mention is made of Sabbath observance for the Christian.

Any talk of the Ten Commandments passing away is treated as heresy, but this is totally missing the point. Jesus fulfilled the law completely, not just a ceremonial law, which is found nowhere in Scripture. The Ten Commandments broadly cover the 613 individual requirements of the law, but they are not separate from it, as tradition teaches. Remembering the Sabbath day, to keep it Holy and do no work, was not the end of that command; God elaborated upon it later. All work was forbidden, including kindling a fire, harvesting, cooking and even gathering sticks; any transgressions would result in the death penalty.

Nobody follows all of these rules today, but Christians who just abstain from work on the Sabbath feel that their watered-down version of keeping this law still fulfils the Fourth Commandment. As previously stated, those who choose to fall back under the Old Covenant are debtors to do the whole law as Christ has become of no effect to them.

When Paul wrote to the churches in Galatia, he was dismayed that they had so quickly fallen into following a gospel other than that taught by the Apostles. Jewish believers who were still following the law were trying to compel the Galatians to do the same and be circumcised, much to the frustration of Paul:

"O foolish Galatians! Who has bewitched you, that you should not obey the truth, before whose eyes Jesus Christ has been evidently set forth, crucified among you?

This only would I learn of you: received you the Spirit by the works of the law, or by the hearing of faith?

Are you so foolish? Having begun in the Spirit, are you now made perfect by the flesh?"

"Even as Abraham 'believed God, and it was accounted to him for righteousness.'

Know you therefore, that they which are of faith, the same are the children of Abraham.

And the scripture, foreseeing that God would justify the heathen through faith, preached before the Gospel unto Abraham, *saying*, 'In you shall all nations be blessed.'

So then, they which be of faith are blessed with faithful Abraham.

For as many as are of the works of the law are under the curse; for it is written, 'Cursed *is* every one that continues not in all things which are written in the book of the law, to do them.'

But that no man is justified by the law in the sight of God *it is* evident, for, 'The just shall live by faith.'

And the law is not of faith, but 'The man that does them shall live in them.'

Christ has redeemed us from the curse of the law, being made a curse for us; for it is written, 'Cursed *is* every one that hangs on a tree'

That the blessing of Abraham might come on the Gentiles through Jesus Christ, that we might receive the promise of the Spirit through faith."

"For if the inheritance *be* of the law, *it is* no more of promise; but God gave *it* to Abraham by promise."

(Galatians 3:1–3, 6–14, 18)

The Ten Commandments are well known, and these "moral laws" are universally accepted by most of the world's religions. There is nothing unusual about these commands as they represent a standard of good behaviour that few would disagree with, apart from the Fourth, which is very specific to belief in the God of the Bible. When the subject of this commandment not being necessary anymore is raised, it is usually dismissed instantly or met with ridicule. "The moral law or Ten Commandments stand forever," they will say. So why would God only uphold nine? "I suppose it's okay to sleep with my neighbour's wife now?" is another response used to mock whoever would question this aspect of the law.

Statements like these are common and show a sad lack of understanding in those who fail to hear and understand the words of Jesus and the Apostles. It is important to re-peat that there is no such thing as "moral and ceremonial law". These are man-made terms that are now taught as gospel but are found nowhere in Scripture. The Ten Com-mandments were given by God as a grand overview of His law, but the people were afraid and pleaded with Moses to hear God no more, lest they should die (Exodus 20:18–19).

Deuteronomy's 18th chapter tells us that God was pleased with Israel's fearful reaction to His presence as this usually reflects respect and obedience, but unfortunately, it didn't take long for them to backslide and become disobedient. God hark-ened to Israel's wishes and went on to give a detailed account of the law for Moses to pass on to the people. These details were an integral part of the Ten Commandments, which made up what became known as the Law of Moses, but can also be seen as the "table of contents" for the book of the law.

After telling us that he has not come to destroy the law or the Prophets, but to fulfil them, Jesus goes on to repeat a phrase several times to show that he was bringing a higher standard of behaviour that built upon the Law of Moses.

"'You have heard that it was said by them of old time, "You shall not kill," and, whosoever shall kill, shall be in danger of the judgement.

'But I say unto you, that whosoever is angry with his brother without a cause, shall be in danger of the judgement.'"

(Matthew 5:21–22)

"'You have heard that it was said by them of old time, "You shall not commit adultery."

'But I say unto you, that whosoever looks on a woman to lust after her, has committed adultery with her already in his heart.'"

(Matthew 5:27–28)

These are just two of many examples where Jesus tries to instil a higher standard upon His followers that established the meaning behind the law, to be written upon their hearts, rather than just following letters, written upon tablets of stone. Every jot and tittle of the Mosaic Law was fulfilled by Jesus, who stated with His final words upon the Cross, "It is finished." From that moment, the true believer could find rest from his labours through faith in the finished work of Christ, with the law now being summed up by one word: "Love".

"Owe no man anything but to love one another, for he that loves another has fulfilled the law.

For this, 'You shall not commit adultery', 'You shall not kill', 'You shall not steal', 'You shall not bear false witness', 'You shall not covet', and if *there be* any other commandment, it is briefly comprehended in this saying, namely, 'You shall love your neighbour as yourself'.

Love works no ill to his neighbour, therefore love *is* the fulfilling of the law."

(Romans 13:8–10)

"For Christ *is* the end of the law for righteousness to anyone that believes."

(Romans 10:4)

When one of the Pharisees, who was a lawyer, questioned Jesus, saying:

"'Master, which *is* the great commandment in the law?'

Jesus said unto him, 'You shall love the LORD your God with all your heart, and with all your soul, and with all your mind.

'This is the first and great commandment.

'And the second *is* like unto it: You shall love your neighbour as yourself.

'On these two commandments hang all the law and the prophets.'"

(Matthew 22:36–40)

Despite these clear teachings that show the simplicity that is in Christ, how love of God and our neighbour fulfils the law, many still overlook these things and put themselves back under the yoke of bondage that Christ came to relieve us from.

Paul's letter to the Romans makes it clear that the day of worship is not an issue, just as eating or not eating certain foods is no longer an issue either. Paul stresses that not everyone would understand these things, so it was important to avoid unnecessary division.

"One man esteems one day above another; another esteems every day *alike*. Let every man be fully persuaded in his own mind.

He that regards the day, regards *it* unto the LORD; and he that regards not the day, to the LORD he does not regard it. He that eats, eats to the LORD, for he gives God thanks; and he that eats not, to the LORD he eats not, and gives God thanks."

"For the kingdom of God is not meat and drink, but righteousness, and peace, and joy in the Holy Ghost.

For he that in these things serves Christ, *is* acceptable to God, and approved of men."

(Romans 14:5–6, 17–18)

There is now no need to abstain from certain foods or to treat any day of the week differently from any other. If you want to set aside a certain day for worship or study, then there is nothing wrong with that, whether it be on Saturday, Sunday or Wednesday; they are all God's, and Satan has no claim over any of them. The Sabbath day, together with the law and the Prophets, pointed to Christ, with God's seventh day rest being a foreshadowing of Christ's millennial reign during the seventh prophetic day of Earth's history.

Rome has taken a traditional meeting day for Christians, that celebrated the day of Christ's Resurrection, and turned it into a replacement Sabbath to honour itself. Just as the Church of Rome continues to overspread abominations by the perpetual sacrifice of Jesus – during the Eucharist of the Catholic Mass – they also negate His finished work upon the Cross by reinstating Sabbath day obligations but on the first day of the week.

The Catholic Church is very happy to point out that it is only the Seventh Day Adventists who uphold the authority of Scripture in regard to the Biblical Sabbath. This appears to be a challenge to Protestants to join that denomination if they truly reject the authority of Rome, a perfect example of controlled opposition! It is no surprise that the Synagogue of Satan would cover all its bases by encouraging everyone to reject Christ's work and go back under the bondage of the law. The problem with Sunday worship is nothing to do with the day; the problem only occurs if you see that day as a replacement Sabbath.

It's sad to see how many Christians still feel a legal obligation to observe the Sabbath through group worship and avoiding certain foods prohibited under the Law of Moses. This was also the case in the early days of the Church, which prompted the Apostles and elders to come together to consider the matter. This meeting became known as the Council of Jerusalem and was held approximately twenty years after the Crucifixion. After carefully considering the issues raised, the Apostles and the Church sent chosen men to Antioch with Paul and Barnabas:

"And they wrote *letters* by them after this manner:

The apostles and elders, and brethren, *send* greeting unto the brethren, which are of the Gentiles in Antioch, and Syria, and Cilicia.

Forasmuch as we have heard, that certain which went out from us, have troubled you with words, subverting your souls, saying, '*You must* be circumcised and keep the law' – to whom we gave no *such* commandment –

it seemed good unto us, being assembled with one accord, to send chosen men unto you, with our beloved Barnabas and Paul, men that have hazarded their lives for the name of our Lord Jesus Christ.

We have sent therefore Judas and Silas, who shall also tell *you* the same things by mouth.

For it seemed good to the Holy Ghost, and to us, to lay upon you no greater burden than these necessary things:

that you abstain from meats offered to idols, and from blood, and from things strangled, and from fornication, from which if you keep yourselves, you shall do well.

Fare you well."

(Acts 15:23–29)

This decree, given by the Apostles, couldn't be more clear, and yet many Christians just ignore it in favour of earlier ordinances that were specifically given to the Jews under the previous covenant that Christ fulfilled. The pride of the Pharisees is all too common, and even today, this attitude persists, which blinds the eyes into only seeing the shadow and not the substance. The Pharisees thought that they were pleasing God by blind legalism, as zealously following ordinances made them feel like they were actively doing something to earn salvation, whilst at the same time, showing no love, forgiveness or compassion towards their fellow man.

Jesus came to fulfil and remove the bondage of the law from our lives, and to replace it with what His brother called the "royal law": that you shall love your neighbour as yourself (James 2:8).

"The fruit of the Spirit is love, joy, peace, long suffering, gentleness, goodness, faith,

Meekness, temperance; against such there is no law."

(Galatians 5:22–23)

"I am crucified with Christ. Nevertheless, I live, yet not I, but Christ lives in me, and the life which I now live in the flesh, I live by the faith of the Son of God, who loved me, and gave himself for me.

I do not frustrate the grace of God; for if righteousness *come* by the law, then Christ is dead in vain."

(Galatians 2:20–21)

1   Jones, A. H. M., *Constantine and the Conversion of Europe*, p.100, Hodder & Stourton Ltd., London. 1948.

CHAPTER XI

THE GREAT END TIMES DECEPTION

Throughout the history of the false church, the Antichrist has constantly worked to subvert the teachings of Scripture that clearly identify it as the Synagogue of Satan. With the founding of the Jesuit order, just prior to the Council of Trent, the Papacy was given the most evil, efficient and far-reaching army the Earth has ever seen.

The Jesuits have worked tirelessly for nearly 500 years to deceive and destroy anyone that would question or hinder the rise and total authority of the Papal Antichrist. One of the most effective weapons in their arsenal has been the control of education and the introduction of false doctrine. The distribution of the Bible amongst the laity could not be stopped following the invention of the printing press, but its message could be put into question. The Jesuits would go on to infiltrate the Protestant Church and introduce false doctrine, bit by bit, to plant tares amongst the wheat, feeding the lusts of those with itching ears and turning them to fables (2 Timothy 4:3–4). These deceptions would cause the Church to be fractured into a thousand denominational pieces as the leaven of Rome began to spread.

The Reformation of the 16th century saw the revival and growth of a school of thought that became known as "historicism", or the historical view to understanding prophecy. The Protestants came to the realisation that the prophecies contained in Scripture, particularly the books of Daniel and Revelation, were being fulfilled in the past, present and future, as these books accurately predicted events in world history, from Babylon until the end of the age when Christ would return.

The name "Protestant" came from the fact that this group clearly identified the Papacy as the Little Horn of Daniel 7 and the Antichrist Man of Sin of Revelation, leading them to "protest" the authority of the Pope over the Church. The newly formed Society of Jesus (or Jesuits) launched an intellectual attack on the doctrines of the reformers to sow doubt and confusion in the hope of turning attention away from the Protestants' identification of the Pope as the Antichrist of Scripture. This Counter-Reformation was started at the Council of Trent, with the Catholic Church and its army of Jesuits vowing to destroy Protestantism and its Bible based on the received text (or Textus Receptus).

In 1590, the Spanish Jesuit, Francisco Ribera, published a commentary on the book of Revelation that became the foundation for most of the futurist doctrines that would follow.[1] Ribera speculated that the Antichrist would be an individual, evil man who would show up just before Christ's return to fulfil all but the first few chapters of the book of Revelation. Ribera thought that this Man of Sin would rebuild the temple in Jerusalem, abolish Christianity, be received by the Jews and go on to destroy Rome and conquer the world.

Ribera's ideas were not entirely new, as several of the early so-called Church Fathers, such as Irenaeus and Hippolytus,[2&3] had put forward theories of a future Antichrist who would show up during Daniel's 70th week, at the end of Earth's history. Just as Paul had predicted, a great falling away from the true gospel, as preached by the Apostles, had begun and would continue for nearly 400 years after their deaths, when the Antichrist was revealed following the apparent fall of the Western Roman Empire under the Caesars.

The Italian Jesuit and Professor of Theology, Cardinal Robert Bellarmine, was in agreement with Ribera and gave many lectures supporting and expanding upon his ideas. He had joined the Society of Jesus in 1560, a few years before the close of the Council of Trent, and became a prolific writer, defending Catholic doctrine over that of the Protestant heretics.

Daniel's 9th chapter ended with a prophecy that charted the exact time of Christ's ministry between 26–33 AD, which was the 70th and final week of years the Jews had been given to bring an end of sins. The Reformers realised that the "He" who should confirm the covenant with many for one week, was referring to Jesus Christ. In the midst of the week, "He" would cause the sacrifice and oblation to cease, a reference to Jesus being crucified three and a half years after his ministry started, and becoming the final sacrifice acceptable to God. The Apostles would continue to spread the gospel to the Jews for another three and a half years to complete Daniel's 70th week of years (or the 490 years) God had given the Jewish nation to end the transgression by accepting their Messiah.

Ribera and Bellarmine twisted this incredible prophecy to make "the Antichrist" the one who would confirm the covenant and cause the sacrifice to cease, by cutting off Daniel's 70th week of years from the other 69 and placing it in the distant future, before Christ's return. This diabolical plan was designed to remove the accusation that Daniel, Paul and John had accurately described the identity, rise and terrible persecutions perpetrated by the Papal Antichrist upon Christendom. Bellarmine was considered a leading figure in the Counter-Reformation, and the work of these two men planted a seed that would eventually grow to choke out the historicist truth that the Pope is the Antichrist.

The next stepping stone on the path to Futurism came when another Jesuit, Manuel de Lacunza, who was born in Santiago, Chile, wrote a book entitled *The Coming of Messiah in Majesty and Glory*. Lacunza wrote his book under the pseudonym, Rabbi Juan Josafat Ben-Ezra, and in 1810 it was secretly published in Spanish. Lacunza gave his interpretation of Daniel and Revelation together with the earlier views of Ribera and Bellarmine, which differed slightly from his own ideas. Lacunza stated that although the Antichrist was future, he would not be an individual, evil man, but a moral apostasy made up of many false religions that would share the Antichrist spirit. In 1819, his book was removed from circulation by the Spanish Inquisition, although further editions continued to be printed in other countries during the next few years. Pope Leo XII placed Lacunza's work on the index of prohibited books in 1824, laying the groundwork for his book to be eagerly gobbled up by gullible Reformers who wanted to get their hands on this hidden truth that the Papacy was suppressing.

Lacunza's work bore all the hallmarks of a Jesuit plot to introduce this false doctrine amongst the Reformers, and in 1827, they succeeded when the Scottish preacher Edward Irving translated and published his book in English. Irving became obsessed with Lacunza's work, and even after discovering that it was written by a Jesuit, and not a converted Jew as he had previously thought, he still followed its teachings – although he was inclined to agree with Ribera and Bellarmine when it came to the Antichrist being a future evil individual.

Irving had been fascinated with prophecy and the Second Advent of Christ for several years before Lacunza's book found its way into his hands. Between 1826 and 1830, he was heavily involved with the Albury Conferences at Albury Park in Surrey, England. These prophetic conferences, attended mainly by Anglican clergy, gave rise to a group that became known as the Albury Circle, who, together with Irving, were instrumental in the founding of the Catholic Apostolic Church, in 1832, also known as the Irvingian Church.

The Albury Conferences gave rise to many ideas that would spread amongst the movements that sprang up shortly after their close. The Millerite Movement started the following year, leading to the founding of the Seventh Day Adventist Church, which believed, as Irving had, that Christ's return was very close. It is interesting to note that, even today, the SDA identifies the 1260-year period spoken of in the book of Revelation to identify the reign of Antichrist as being between the Decree of Justinian and the French Revolution, an idea promoted at Albury.

Irving believed that there would be a great outpouring of the Holy Spirit before Christ's return and that his parishioners should pray for spiritual gifts such as healing, prophesying and speaking in tongues, and they would be returned to the Church. Shortly after this, there were reports of miraculous events, such as those just listed, occurring in another Scottish church that Irving was associated with, causing much excitement at the final Albury Conference in 1830. A fifteen-year-old Scottish girl called Margaret MacDonald was said to have received visions of a "Secret Rapture" of the Church before that Wicked was to be revealed – a reference to the Antichrist coming to reign for seven years after the Holy Spirit, who was restraining his rise, was taken out of the way. Christ was then to return again at the end of the seven years – a "second Second Coming" – to defeat the Antichrist; a doctrine that became known as the Pretribulation Rapture.

The Irvingian Church was following doctrines borrowed from the Jesuits, the very agents of the Antichrist. Jesus stated that a bad tree cannot bring forth good fruit, so are we to believe that God would impart the same spiritual gifts upon its members that He gave to the Apostles? I think not!

Irving was excommunicated by the presbytery of London and removed from the ministry of the Church of Scotland in 1833, due to his strange practices and heretical teachings on the sinful nature of Christ; he would die the following year. The ideas and practises of Edward Irving and his followers can be seen today in the Pentecostal and charismatic movements that are spreading worldwide, but particularly in America, as signs and lying wonders are leading millions astray.

This was an extremely dangerous time for the Church, as Satan launched a full-scale onslaught upon the truths that had been returned to God's people during the Reformation. Around the time that Irving was translating Lacunza's book, two other men, Dr S. R. Maitland, librarian to the Archbishop of Canterbury, and James H. Todd, a professor of Hebrew at Dublin University, began publishing books and pamphlets supporting the futurist, individual Antichrist ideas of Ribera and Bellarmine.

In England, the Anglican priest and theologian John Henry Newman was working hard behind the scenes to return the Church of England to the ritualistic Catholic beliefs that were common before the Reformation. The "Oxford Movement", named after the university where Newman and most of his followers studied, ran between 1833–1845 and caused tremendous damage to the Church by undoing much of the work of the great men of the Reformation who had given their lives to expose the evil deceptions of the Church of Rome. Newman left the Church of England and converted to Catholicism in 1845; Pope Leo XIII ordained him as a cardinal in 1879 due to his hard work furthering the cause of the Catholic Church in England. In 2019, Cardinal and now Saint John Henry Newman was canonised after being approved by Pope Francis; as always, the Antichrist mother church greatly rewards her loyal children!

In 1831, the year following the final Albury Conference, John Nelson Darby became a prominent speaker at the annual Powerscourt Conferences in Ireland, which were organised by his friend Lady Powerscourt, who had attended the Albury meetings. Darby was born in Westminster, England, to an Anglo-Irish family. In his mid-20s, he became a priest in the Anglican Church of Ireland, with a parish in County

Wicklow, the home of Powerscourt. He spent much of his time converting the local Catholic peasants until a rift with the Archbishop of Dublin, who ruled that converts were to swear allegiance to George IV as rightful King of Ireland, caused him to resign in protest.

In 1827, Darby was seriously injured following a riding accident, and during his recovery he developed his ideas that Israel and the Church were two separate entities for which God had distinctly different plans. Israel was seen as a purely ethnic nation, whereas the Church consisted of all those who were saved from the time that the gospel went out to the Gentiles until the Rapture that would occur before the Tribulation. The earthly program, or dispensation for the kingdom promise of Israel, would be put on hold for the Church Age, which would continue when the Church was raptured out of the way; this was the separated 70th week of Daniel (or "Gap") that had been developed over 200 years earlier by the Jesuits.

For thousands of years, God had been preparing His people for the coming of their Messiah through the law and the Prophets he had sent to them. Following Christ's death, which was the final sacrifice acceptable to God, salvation was available to both Jew and Gentile through faith that His finished work upon the Cross had paid the price for our sins and the free gift of grace would be given to those who believed. The Israel of God now consisted of the true believers in His Son; Gentiles could be grafted into the natural olive tree, which was once Israel in the flesh, due to branches of the natural tree being broken off through unbelief. When Jews, through faith, accepted that Jesus was their Messiah, they would be grafted back in to form the true Church – Christ's two witnesses, both Jew and Gentile (Romans 11:1–24).

The dispensationalist view that God has an earthly plan for national Israel and a heavenly one for the Church is totally misguided. The Church is the Israel of God who will be part of the first resurrection, to reign with Christ on Earth for a thousand years and not be subject to the second death due to their faith in Him before His return (Revelation 20:4–6). National Israel will not be regathered by God until they accept Christ, as the only way to the Father is through the Son. When Christ returns, every eye shall see Him and they will look upon Him who they pierced and there will be a great mourning in Jerusalem, only then will God restore them to the promised land (Zechariah 12).

After becoming disillusioned with the organised church, Darby joined a group of likeminded believers who would get together to discuss and develop their ideas; they became known as the Plymouth Brethren, after the town where their first meeting in England was held. The brethren were heavily influenced by the conferences at Albury and Powerscourt, and it is likely that Darby and Irving met and corresponded during the first Powerscourt Conference in 1831, or possibly a smaller, unofficial one the year before.

There is much debate as to which man came up with the Pretribulation Rapture theory and the separate "dispensations" for the Church and Israel, as their ideas were so similar. It is highly likely that Darby was already thinking along similar lines as Irving and went on to develop some of Darby's ideas and claim them as his own, something he was known to have done with several ideas put forward at Al-

THE GREAT END TIMES DECEPTION

bury. Darby's later success probably led his followers to try to distance him from Irving, to promote Darby's teachings as original, rather than built on the ideas of others. This was made easier by the death of Irving in 1834, the year following the last Powerscourt Conference.

Over the next fifty years, Darby would travel all over Europe, Canada and America, teaching his theories, writing commentaries (including a translation of the New Testament in 1867) and setting up assemblies of Brethren. Today, Darby is credited as being the Father of Dispensationalism and the originator of the Pretribulation Rapture, when in reality, he just developed and popularised earlier ideas.

John Nelson Darby died in 1882, and the following year, the American lawyer and Politician, Cyrus Ingerson Scofield, was ordained as a minister. Scofield had joined the Confederate Army as a teenager and fought in the Civil War before his relatively short career in law and politics. He was a controversial figure, having been divorced by his wife due to neglect of both her and their children, together with many other scandals including bribery and forgery, which he was later jailed for. Much of his life is a mystery, with many discrepancies regarding things he claimed to have done being unsubstantiated, such as his Doctor of Divinity degree.

Scofield was apparently converted to evangelical Christianity by a lawyer friend, before being tutored and guided by the Rev James H. Brookes in St Louis, Missouri. Brookes was known to be one of the founding fathers of Dispensationalism in America after adopting and promoting the doctrines of John Nelson Darby and the Plymouth Brethren. More than anyone else, it was Scofield who would promote and popularise the ideas of Darby, in the same way that Darby had built upon the teachings of Irving.

In 1888, Scofield published his first work, a short book entitled *Rightly Dividing the Word of Truth*, which put forward the dispensationalist viewpoint. 2 Timothy 2:15, which ends with the statement he used for his book title, was totally misrepresented by Scofield. The full verse starts by stating: "Study to show yourself approved unto God, a workman that needs not to be ashamed." Rightly dividing the word of truth actually refers to the fact that God has hidden the full meaning of certain teachings within multiple books of the Bible, and that it is up to us to diligently search the scriptures, as the Bereans did, to make these connections and come to the knowledge of the truth. A perfect example of this is the twin books of Daniel and Revelation that work together with Paul's letter to the Thessalonians to identify the Little Horn, Man of Sin, the Papal Antichrist.

Proverbs 25:2 states that "it is the glory of God to conceal a thing, but the honour of kings is to search out a matter." Scofield twisted this great truth to sell the futurist lie of Dispensationalism to the vast majority of the Christian world, who are happy to trust in man's interpretation of Scripture, even when it contradicts Scripture itself.

In 1887, Scofield attended the Niagara Bible Conference, followed by many others all over the United States. These conferences, focusing mainly on prophecy, were just a continuation of the conferences held in the United Kingdom at Albury and Powerscourt, where Irving and Darby had successfully planted the futurist seed that quickly grew and spread to America via the Plymouth Brethren.

As discussed in Chapter II, 1881 saw a deadly blow inflicted upon the true word of God, when a revision was made to the King James Bible by men whose ideology was in line with that of the Vatican. Despite this attack, the King James Bible survived, but Cyrus Scofield was to inflict an equally deadly blow when, in 1909, he published the work he would become most famous for: the Scofield Reference Bible. Scofield's Bible would become the most popular reference Bible of all time, and the first to print a commentary alongside the actual text since the Geneva Bible of 1560. This new work mixed the Holy with the profane by using the King James Version of the Bible together with Scofield's commentary and references to completely distort the true message of Scripture. Scofield's Bible deceived its readers into accepting the lie of Dispensationalism, the Pretribulation Rapture and a future, separated 70th week of Daniel when the Antichrist would appear.

Darby and Scofield have become trusted household names amongst millions of Christians today, despite their seven-year Pretribulation Rapture teachings being found nowhere in Scripture but having clear roots in the Jesuit Counter-Reformation. The emphasis on a national Israel, rather than a spiritual one, led to the Christian Zionist movement, which worked to bring about the nation state of Israel, which they felt had to come before Christ would return. This forced, false fulfilment of prophecy can easily be identified from Scripture, as the promised regathering of Israel by God does not correspond with what we are seeing today.

In 1924, the Dallas Theological Seminary (DTS) was founded by two brothers, Rollin Thomas Chafer and Lewis

Sperry Chafer. DTS continues to this day, teaching and promoting the dispensation theology of both Darby and Scofield, who died in 1921.

One of the most well-known graduates to come out of DTS is Hal Lindsey, who became known amongst Christians worldwide due to his best-selling book, *The Late Great Planet Earth*. Published in 1970 by Zondervan (owned by Papal Knight Rupert Murdoch), Lindsey's book was said to be the best-selling "non-fiction" book of the 1970s; the truth is, it was pure fiction based on deceptions orchestrated centuries before by the Jesuits. Lindsey was a firm dispensationalist and Christian Zionist, and his book promoted these ideas, together with the Pretribulation Rapture, capturing the imaginations of millions of Christians worldwide. Christianity had become distorted to such an extent that it was barely recognisable when compared to the gospel of the 1st century.

In 1995, the first of a series of fictional novels that came to be known as the *Left Behind* series, after the name of the first novel, was published by Tim LaHaye and Jerry B. Jenkins. *Left Behind* charts the rise of a future, single Antichrist who appears at the beginning of a seven-year tribulation period following a "secret rapture" when true believers in Christ are instantly removed from the Earth. The series has successfully sold an entire generation (which was brought up in an age of fantasy and science-fiction) on the false doctrines of Dispensationalism, Futurism and a Pretribulation Rapture. Although fictional, the books planted the idea in the minds of millions of Christians that the end time events will follow a very similar path to that of the novels, especially as these doctrines are universally taught by most so-called Protestant denominations.

The Pretribulation Rapture theory wasn't just designed to hide the identity of the Antichrist by placing him in the distant future; it also has a more insidious purpose. The majority of Christians today believe that when the great tribulation comes, they will be raptured off the Earth and will avoid the horrors that await those who remain when the Antichrist sets up his kingdom. Nothing could be further from the truth. The New Testament teaches, and history shows, that Christians always have and always will suffer tribulation and persecution – and the end times will be no different!

Paul's letter to the Thessalonians tells us that the Antichrist will be destroyed at Christ's Second Coming; Daniel stated that the Antichrist will make war with the Saints and prevail against them until the Ancient of Days came; and finally, Revelation tells us that he will make war against Christ's two witnesses and shall overcome them and kill them, with their dead bodies lying in the street of the Great City. This final warning describes the symbolic destruction of the true Church in the eyes of the Antichrist, and this will happen three and a half years before they are witnessed ascending to heaven in a cloud, just prior to the sounding of the seventh trumpet, as described in Revelation 11:11–12. Paul's first letter to the Corinthians identifies this moment as the time when all those who are still alive in Christ will be transformed in the twinkling of an eye to meet Christ in the air, and that it happens "after the tribulation of those days", as confirmed by Jesus in Matthew 24:29–31.

As the war against the Saints intensifies, when the Antichrist Popes' 1260-year reign is coming to an end, the ecumenical movement will have united the majority of Christians to believe that Jesus will return to save them. When this doesn't happen, the faith of many will be tested beyond breaking point; their spiritual foundations will begin to crumble with:

"men's hearts failing them for fear and for looking after those things which are coming on the earth; for the powers of heaven shall be shaken.

And then shall they see the Son of man coming in a cloud with power and great glory."

(Luke 21:26–27)

The Jesuits have always sought to unite Protestantism into following false doctrines that lead them away from the truths contained in their Bibles based on the received text. The ecumenical movement was orchestrated to bring different denominations together to find common ground, with the Vatican constantly working in the background, chipping away bit by bit to break down barriers and unite these "separated brethren" to follow doctrines acceptable to "Mother Church".

All of the efforts just explained were designed for one purpose: to hide the accusation from Scripture that the Papacy is the Antichrist. When it is no longer seen in this regard, those churches that previously protested the authority of the Pope become open to making amends for their "mistake" by joining together with their fellow Christians to break bread with the Great Harlot. Satan's plan through the false church is to destroy Christianity from within, to subvert its teachings so the followers of Christ have no idea who He actually is and are blinded to the warnings He gave for the future.

The ecumenical movement, which is the brainchild of Rome, is all about unity. On the surface, unity appears to be a good thing, but not if it is a house built on sand; the only unity of value is that which is founded on the rock that is Christ.

The happy-clappy charismatic movement of today's Christian churches is all about acceptance of everything and everyone. Sins and perversions are welcomed with open arms as the churches virtue signal to themselves and the world that they stand for goodness, love and inclusivity. The truth has no place in the modern Church; the only thing that matters is that you are made to feel like a good person. "God knows my heart," they say, so following God's wishes and instructions as laid out in the Bible becomes unimportant; they rely on corrupted pastors for spiritual guidance instead of the word of God. When Jesus was faced with sinners, He forgave them – but under the condition that they went away and sinned no more. This model has been adapted to enable sinners to continue in their ways; the Church is now flexible and moves with the world in order to be accepted.

Daniel predicted that the Antichrist power would cast the truth to the ground and that it would practise and prosper until the indignation was accomplished; for that which is determined shall be done. Daniel's prophecies started in Babylon and followed through to the end of days. Paul warned that the Man of Sin would be revealed following a falling away from the true faith, and Daniel charted the 1260 years of his reign, following him reaching full power, and the persecutions and deceptions that ensued. Jesus said "I am the way, the truth and the life" because truth is important; truth is reality, and without it, you are living a lie. The Bible tells us that the Devil is the Father of Lies because there is no truth in him, but the Christian of today chooses to walk in his footsteps because it is easier to see the world as they want it to be, by accepting comfortable lies rather than accept the inconvenient and often painful truth.

George Orwell stated that "in a time of universal deceit, telling the truth is a revolutionary act" and that "the further a society drifts from the truth, the more it will hate those that speak it"; we are living in these times now.

Jesus said: "And you shall know the truth and the truth shall make you free." It is better to be free, to fly above a world of lies, than to be like an ostrich with your head buried in the sand you are building your spiritual house upon if you avoid seeking the truth. Jesus foresaw the result of this deception when he stated in Luke 18:8: "when the Son of Man comes, shall he find faith on the earth?"

In these last days, as knowledge increases, many people are turning to alternative sources to seek out the truth, which, in turn, can be tested against the word of God. I hope that this book will play some small part in that awakening and that people will take the example of the Bereans, searching the Scriptures daily to see if those things were so, proving all things and holding fast that which is good.

The fate of Satan and the Antichrist has already been sealed, but their goal is to get as many souls as possible to share their punishment.

"And I heard another voice from heaven saying, 'Come out of her, my people,

that you be not partakers of her sins, and that you receive not of her plagues.'"

(Revelation 18:4)

1   Ribera, Francisco, *In Sacrum Beati Ioannis Apostoli, &*
    Evangelistiae Apocalypsin Commentarii. 1590AD.

2   Irenaeus of Smyrna, *Against Heresies*, book 5, chapter
    25. c.180AD.

3   Hippolytus of Rome, *Treatise on Christ and Antichrist.*
    c.203AD.

CHAPTER XII

THE END OF DAYS AND A NEW BEGINNING

In the previous chapter, we saw how the Jesuits introduced false doctrines surrounding the end times into the Church, leaving Christians open to a huge deception as we approach the prophesied return of Christ. The vast majority of Christians today have their beliefs dictated to them as they follow a curriculum of false teachings that originate from the Church of Rome – the Great Harlot of Revelation – leading its followers away from the true gospel.

If we have been lied to about the events of the last days, then what is the truth, and does Scripture even tell us these things? The Bible is a handbook that gives us all the information we need to navigate this increasingly complicated life, and God has not left us unprepared for what is to come. Like any other set of instructions, the Bible was written for our benefit and was designed to help us avoid making costly mistakes, so it needs to be read carefully and understood. Not everything in Scripture is laid out in order for us to just follow. I believe that God wants us to study His word and make the connections He left for us in order to gain a greater understanding and see the full picture. Jesus often talked in parables for this same reason; he wants us to look more deeply into the message He was trying to portray, to have a changed heart rather than just blindly follow His instructions.

The purpose of this chapter is not to state how the end times will play out, as nobody can know this for sure. All we can do is try to make the connections given throughout Scripture – both Old and New Testaments – to identify a narrative that gives a possible explanation of these events.

The book of Revelation is a complete mystery to many people as its symbolic language can be quite confusing, but when it is read alongside the Prophets of the Old Testament, particularly Daniel, it suddenly starts to make more sense. This final book of Scripture was called Revelation for a reason, as it reveals the missing information to many unanswered questions from the Old Testament. Many Christians believe that the New Testament is their book and the Old Testament was strictly for the Jews. This is a huge mistake because the whole Bible contains God's plan for the salvation of mankind, with the New Testament detailing the fulfilment by Christ of the prophecies contained in the Old. Answers are meaningless unless you have the questions to go with them, and it is the Old Testament that poses these questions. The Jews are lost and left desolate because they turned their backs on Christ, who was the fulfilment of their faith, whereas many Christians are lost and left open to being deceived due to having answers that are not fully understood because the foundation of their faith is missing.

The following chapters rely heavily on quotes from Scripture, as all of these things were foretold in the Old Testament writings of the Prophets. Because many people overlook the Old Testament, they will never get the full picture, so I feel it is important to gather these prophecies, which are scattered throughout the scriptures, and group them together in sections that are relevant to the end times events they fulfil.

The first detailed discussion of the end times in the gospels is Matthew's account of the Olivet Discourse, where Jesus is asked:

"'[...] when shall these things be? And what shall be the sign of your coming, and of the end of the world?'"

(Matthew 24:3)

Jesus tells them that:

"'Immediately after the tribulation of those days shall the sun be darkened, and the moon shall not give her light, and the stars shall fall from heaven, and the powers of the heavens shall be shaken.

'And then shall appear the sign of the Son of man in heaven, and then shall all the tribes of the earth mourn, and they shall see the Son of man coming in the clouds of heaven with power and great glory.

'And he shall send his angels with a great sound of a trumpet, and they shall gather together his elect from the four winds, from one end of heaven to the other."

(Matthew 24:29–31)

Without knowledge of the writings in the Old Testament, many Christians are unaware that Jesus was talking about the great day of the LORD that was foretold by many of the Prophets. Isaiah spoke of the day of the LORD that would come with wrath and fierce anger with the sun being darkened and the moon not causing her light to shine (Isaiah 13:9–10); Joel told of the great and terrible day of the LORD, saying that the sun would be turned into darkness and the moon into blood before that day came (Joel 2:31).

Joel also talked of the Valley of Jehoshaphat, where the men of war from the heathen nations would be gathered by God in the valley of decision, where He would plead with them for His people Israel and judge them for their wickedness. This was a reference to the battle of Armageddon, as we shall see later on.

"Put you in the sickle, for the harvest is ripe.

Come, get you down;

For the press is full,

The vats overflow;

For their wickedness *is* great."

(Joel 3:13)

Revelation 14:19 also gives an account of these events when it states:

"And the angel thrust in his sickle into the earth, and gathered the vine of the earth, and cast it into the great winepress of the wrath of God."

In order to gain understanding of the end times, we have to study the whole of Scripture; the book of Revelation only provides answers when combined with the earlier writings of the Prophets. The chapter on the seven seals identified that we are currently living in the latter stages of the fifth seal, a time of persecution and tribulation that will increase, leading to a time of trouble such as never was, before the sixth seal is opened (Daniel 12:1, Matthew 24:21–30, Mark 13:19–26, Luke 21:24–27). When the sixth seal is opened, there are great signs in the heavens, the sun will become black as sackcloth of hair, the moon as blood and the stars of heaven will fall (Revelation 6:12–17).

As previously stated, this event comes before the great and terrible day of the LORD, and marks the start of his judgements against the wicked:

"And they shall go into the holes of the rocks,

And into the caves of the earth,

For fear of the LORD,

And for the glory of his majesty,

When he arises to shake terribly the earth."

(Isaiah 2:19)

This description also perfectly mirrors the final events that follow the opening of the sixth seal.

In the introduction to this book, I stated that I believe we are entering the time Matthew's 24th chapter describes as the beginning of sorrows, when the Antichrist will speed up his agenda to deceive the nations, destroy our freedoms and ultimately kill those who hold to the true gospel. Only Christ's return will put an end to this evil.

"And except those days should be shortened, there should no flesh be saved; but for the elect's sake those days shall be shortened."

(Matthew 24:22)

The end times events can be divided into five stages. First, we have the tribulation period, which gradually increases in intensity as the final stage of the Antichrist's kingdom is set up upon the Earth. Secondly, we have the battle of Armageddon, the great and terrible day of the LORD, where God will bring the wicked to battle against Israel and Jerusalem; He will destroy Mystery, Babylon the Great, and Satan will be bound for 1000 years. Thirdly we will have the millennial reign of Christ on Earth, where a remnant of Jews will be saved, together with the Saints who had believed in him prior to his return. The fourth stage will be the release of Satan to deceive the nations once more, leading to the final battle of Gog and Magog, where Satan is given his last opportunity to overcome God's people.

Finally, we will have the fifth stage: Satan's armies will be defeated, and the dead who were not part of the first resurrection will be judged; God will make a new heaven and a new earth, and New Jerusalem, the Eternal Kingdom, will descend out of heaven.

CHAPTER XIII

TRIBULATION

The tribulation (or great tribulation) is one of the most misunderstood aspects of the end times.

Previously, in chapter XI, we saw how the Jesuits revived earlier teachings from the so-called Church Fathers to influence the theology of many leading Protestant ministers, who introduced these false teachings amongst their followers. A separated, future 70th week of Daniel became a seven-year tribulation period, with Jesus returning to rapture the Saints from the Earth before the tribulation starts, so they would avoid the horrors that would be unleashed. During this time, the Antichrist would rise to power to sign a seven-year peace deal with Israel in a rebuilt third temple, only to break the "covenant" three and a half years later. This would lead to three and a half years of great tribulation, culminating in the battle of Armageddon, where Christ would return with the Saints who had been raptured.

There is nothing in this account that is backed up by Scripture; it is based entirely upon a terrible misreading of Daniel 9:24–27. The end of Daniel's 9th chapter gives a perfect description of the fulfilment of Daniel's 70ᵗʰ week by Jesus Christ, giving us a detailed account of His ministry and death, and the consequences of these momentous events, hundreds of years before they took place! The truth about this incredible prophecy cannot be overstated, as the deception surrounding it is leading millions of Christians down the broad path to destruction.

Daniel 9:24 tells us that seventy weeks were determined upon Daniel's people (the Jews) and upon his holy city (Jerusalem) to finish the transgression, make an end of sins, make reconciliation for iniquity, bring in everlasting righteousness, seal up the vision and the prophecy, and anoint the Most Holy. The seventy weeks were actually seventy weeks of years (or 490 years), as we have seen previously. God gave the Jews this period of time to return to Him and to start following His ways and commandments.

When Peter asked Jesus how often he should forgive his brothers' sins against him:

"Jesus said unto him, 'I say not unto you, until seven times, but until seventy times seven."

(Matthew 18:22)

Here we see a direct reference to Daniel's prophecy and how Jesus Himself was the embodiment of God's willingness to forgive His people seventy times seven times. Not only this, it also confirms that it was Christ who fulfilled Daniel's 70ᵗʰ week between 26 AD and 33 AD, and not the Antichrist in the long distant future.

Daniel 9:25 tells how God was to mark the start of the 70ᵗʰ week of years by sending His Son, "Messiah the Prince", to start His ministry precisely on time; seven weeks

and threescore and two weeks (or 483 years) after the decree by Artaxerxes was given to restore and build Jerusalem
in 458BC. Daniel 9:26 informs us that after the threescore
and two weeks that followed the initial seven weeks, Messiah
would be cut off, but not for Himself. Daniel 9:27 gives us
extra details about this when it states:

"And He shall confirm the covenant with many for one
week; and in the midst of the week, He shall cause the sacrifice and the oblation to cease."

The covenant spoken of here was the New (and better)
Covenant that Christ was bringing in His own flesh:

"For God so loved the world, that he gave his only begot-
ten Son, that whosoever believes in him should not perish
but have everlasting life."

(John 3:16)

All the Jews had to do to end the transgression was to
accept their Messiah; in other words, to anoint the Most Holy
and bring in everlasting righteousness. Doing this would
have made reconciliation for iniquity and sealed up the vision
and prophecy, but it wasn't to be.

Jesus's ministry started in the autumn of 26AD when he
was baptised by John in the Jordan river; three and a half
years later, Jesus died on the Cross, cut off not for Himself but for the sins of us all. The sacrifices and oblations of
the Old Covenant ceased to be recognised by God, who had
Himself provided the final sacrificial lamb – as promised to
Abraham – the only one that would be acknowledged from
that day on.

Although the Jews continued to sacrifice after Christ
paid the price for sin, God turned a blind eye to this abom-

ination as He had promised to give them three and a half more years to end the final week, realise their mistake and repent. During this second half of Daniel's 70th week, the Apostles continued to preach the gospel to the Jews to give them every opportunity to end the transgression, culminating in Steven's impassioned plea to them, which resulted in his rejection and death.

Jesus foretold these things in His parable of the wicked tenants, where the householder who planted the vineyard sent his servants to the tenants to receive the fruits thereof. One by one, the servants were beaten or killed, just as the Prophets were when God sent them into the world that he had planted. Last of all, the householder:

"'sent his son unto them saying, "they will respect my son."

'But when they saw the son they said amongst themselves, "This is the heir; come, let us kill him and let us seize his inheritance."'"

Jesus ended His prophetic parable by stating:

"'Therefore I say unto you, the kingdom of God shall be taken from you and given to a nation bringing forth the fruits thereof.'"

(Matthew 21:33–44)

After Steven's plea at the end of the 70th week was rejected, the continuation of the sacrificial system was the overspreading of abominations that would bring about the 2300 years of desolation spoken of in Daniel's 8th chapter. Jerusalem would be left desolate, together with its people, until the consummation (or end of days), when that determined should be poured upon the desolate. The gospel now went out to the Gentiles in perfect fulfilment of Jesus's warning to the Jews, as we have just seen.

The futurist lies that have twisted this amazing prophecy have led directly to the huge seven-year tribulation and Pretribulation Rapture deception that has spread like wildfire throughout the Church. The covenant of Daniel 9:27 has become a peace deal that the Antichrist would make with Israel, and in the midst of the week, the Antichrist would put an end to the restored sacrificial system in a rebuilt third temple. You have to perform some incredible mental gymnastics in order to separate the 70th week of years from the other sixty-nine and put it over 2000 years in the future, then swap Christ with the Antichrist, but this hasn't stopped countless millions of Christians from believing this nonsense.

Whilst a great many Christians are comforted by the idea that they will be raptured off the Earth before the tribulation, the Bible paints a completely different picture. The history of Christ's Church is one of continuous persecution and tribulation, as God's people have willingly endured torture and death in order to stand for truth. Jesus said that we would be delivered up to be afflicted, to be killed and hated of all nations, but also that those who would lose their life for His sake would find it.

When Paul wrote to the Philippians he stated:

"For unto you it is given in the behalf of Christ, not only to believe on him, but also to suffer for his sake."

(Philippians 1:29)

The faith of many will be tested beyond breaking point if they believe they will be raptured away to avoid suffering tribulation. God didn't allow Christians to suffer enormous persecution for 2000 years only to care about the final generation in the last days. There will be a catching away when the dead in Christ are resurrected to meet Him in the air, followed by those believers who are still living, but this occurs as the last trumpet is sounded and "after" the tribulation.

In Revelation 11, the two witnesses (or the Jewish and Gentile believers in Christ) are all but wiped out as the followers of the Antichrist celebrate their demise for three and a half days (or three and a half years in prophecy). After these three and a half years:

"[...] the Spirit of life from God entered into them, and they stood upon their feet; and great fear fell upon them which saw them.

And they heard a great voice from heaven saying unto them, 'Come up here.' And they ascended up to heaven in a cloud, and their enemies beheld them."

(Revelation 11:11–12)

A parallel verse to this is 1 Thessalonians 5:3, which states:

"For when they shall say, 'Peace and safety!' then sudden destruction comes upon them, as travail upon a woman with child; and they shall not escape."

Those who celebrated the apparent destruction of Christianity experience great fear as the believers in Christ ascend to meet Him in the air, and those who are left face the third woe, the seven last plagues of the wrath of God (Revelation 11:14 & 15:1). All this happens just prior to the seventh trumpet, so it is clear that the inhabitants of Earth will suffer the great tribulation of the previous six trumpet judgements, not to mention the tribulation of the time of the fifth seal, which we are living in now.

It has to be remembered that in the book of Revelation we have seven seals being opened, which represent seven divisions of Earth's history, as discussed in Chapter VI. This is followed by seven trumpets being sounded, and finally, we have the seven vials of God's justice being poured out upon the desolate. When the sixth seal is opened, the sun and moon are darkened – the event described in Matthew 24:29 as happening immediately after the tribulation of those days.

In Revelation chapter 7, John describes the sealing of the 144,000, after which he beholds:

"a great multitude, which no man could number, of all nations, and kindreds, and peoples, and tongues, stood before the throne, and before the Lamb, clothed with white robes, and palms in their hands."

(Revelation 7:9)

Revelation chapter 6 tells us how John witnesses the opening of the fifth seal and sees the souls of them that were slain for the Word of God, and for the testimony that they held. White robes were given unto every one of them and they were told that they should rest until their fellow servants and brethren should be killed as they were, speaking of the continued tribulation that will be experienced by the Saints "before" Christ's return.

After John describes the great multitudes clothed in white robes, one of the elders tells him that they are the ones who came out of the great tribulation and have washed their robes and made them white in the blood of the Lamb. This speaks of how they endured the tribulation, not avoided it, and how they held true to Jesus throughout their ordeal, having their sins washed away by the shed blood of Christ, as Isaiah prophesied:

"'Come now, and let us reason together,'

Says the LORD,

'Though your sins be as scarlet,

'They shall be as white as snow;

'Though they be red like crimson,

'They shall be as wool.'"

(Isaiah 1:18)

Jesus's life was an example to us all of how God wants us to live our lives. He patiently suffered persecution and turned the other cheek, teaching us that love is the fulfilment of the law.

"'These things I have spoken unto you, that in me you might have peace. In the world you shall have tribulation; but be of good cheer, I have overcome the world.'"

(John 16:33)

Paul wrote, in his letter to the Romans, that they "Be not overcome of evil, but overcome evil with good." John wrote that "Whatsoever is born of God overcomes the world; and this is the victory that overcomes the world, even our faith."

There is a pattern throughout the New Testament where Jesus teaches us to love our enemies and that we will suffer for our faith. The Pretribulation Rapture theory destroys this message and makes the Christian of today complacent and unprepared to suffer as their brethren have in the past. When Jesus tells John what to write to the seven churches in Asia at the beginning of the book of Revelation, he confirms this message seven times by ending each letter with a general message to us all.

To the Church of Ephesus:

"To him that overcomes will I give to eat of the tree of life, which is in the midst of the paradise of God."

To the Church in Smyrna:

"He that overcomes shall not be hurt of the second death."

To the Church in Pergamum:

"To him that overcomes will I give to eat of the hidden manna, and will give him a white stone, and in the stone a new name written, which no man knows except him who receives it."

To the Church in Thyatira:

"And he that overcomes and keeps my works unto the end, to him will I give power over the nations; and I will give him the morning star."

To the Church in Sardis:

"He that overcomes, the same shall be clothed in white clothing; and I will not blot out his name out of the book of life, but I will confess his name before my Father and before his angels."

To the Church of Philadelphia:

"Him that overcomes, will I make a pillar in the temple of my God, and he shall go no more out; and I will write upon him the name of my God, and the name of the city of my God, which is New Jerusalem, which comes down out of heaven from my God; and I will write upon him my new name."

To the Church of the Laodiceans:

"To him that overcomes, will I grant to sit with me in my throne, even as I also overcame, and am sat down with my Father in his throne."

He that has an ear, let him hear what the Spirit says unto the churches!

CHAPTER XIV

THE BATTLE OF ARMAGEDDON

The battle of Armageddon represents God's final judgement upon those who have turned their backs on Him and have chosen to follow the beast. We have seen how we are now living in the period of the fifth seal, a time of persecution and tribulation that is still ongoing. When the sixth seal is opened, we will see great signs in the heavens, with the sun becoming black as sackcloth and the moon as blood, the event Jesus foretold would come after the tribulation and before his Second Coming.

When the seventh seal is opened, the angels are given the seven trumpets, which announce seven plagues upon the Earth. It should be noted that Christians will be living through this period, which is already after the great tribulations of the fifth seal.

It is not until the seventh trumpet is sounded that the dead in Christ will be raised to meet Him in the air, immediately followed by those still living, as we see in Matthew 24:29–31, Mark 13:24–27, Luke 21:25–27, Acts 2:20–21, 1 Corinthians 15:51–52, 1 Thessalonians 4:15–17 and

Revelation 11:11–12. After the seventh trumpet sounds, seven angels are given seven vials, which are the seven last plagues, for in them is completed the wrath of God (Revelation 15:1). These plagues increase until the sixth vial is poured out and God gathers together the nations that oppose him into a place called, in the Hebrew tongue, Armageddon. When the seventh vial is poured out, we will have reached the end of days and a new beginning as Christ sets up His millennial kingdom upon the Earth.

There is no literal place today called Armageddon, which is a Greek translation of the Hebrew *har-megiddo* (Mount Megiddo), *har-megiddon* (the mount of the assembly) or, interestingly, *chormah-gedehon* (the destruction of their army). Megiddo is situated in northern Israel, overlooking the entrance to its northern mountains from the Valley of Jezreel. In Joel chapter 3, God states that He will gather all nations and bring them down into the Valley of Jehoshaphat, which He later calls "the valley of decision", where He will sit to judge the heathen round about.

Jehoshaphat was the fourth king of Judah, and his name means "Yahweh has judged" – a perfect fit for the judgement of the nations who will gather together to make war against Him that sat on the horse, and against His army (Revelation 19:19).

In the 26th chapter of the book of Leviticus, God warned His people that if they didn't follow His judgements, statutes and commandments, and broke their covenant with Him, He would set His face against them and they would be given over to their enemies and scattered amongst the heathen nations. Following this grave warning, God tells them that if they confess their iniquity and the iniquity of their fathers, then He would remember His covenant with Jacob, Isaac and Abraham, and a remnant would be saved (Isaiah 10:20–22).

Time and time again, the Jews broke their covenant with God, provoking Him to anger and leading Him to send Gabriel to the Prophet Daniel with a final warning. Seventy weeks of years were determined upon Daniel's people to end the transgression and bring in everlasting righteousness, but they failed, which led to them being scattered among the nations, just as God warned. The indignation was prophesied to last 2300 years, as we see in Daniel 8:14, until God intervenes to put an end to the plight of His people and to punish the nations that revelled in their suffering.

"And in that day you shall say:

'O LORD, I will praise you;

Though you were angry with me,

Your anger is turned away, and you comforted me.'"

(Isaiah 12:1)

Throughout the writings of the Prophets, we hear mention of the great and terrible day of the LORD, where He will put an end to the punishment of His people and bring retribution on all the nations of Earth who will come against Jerusalem.

"'Therefore wait you upon me,' says the LORD,

'Until the day that I rise up to the prey;

'For my determination *is* to gather the nations,

'That I may assemble the kingdoms,

'To pour upon them my indignation,

'*Even* all my fierce anger;

'For all the earth shall be devoured

'With the fire of My jealousy.'"

(Zephaniah 3:8)

This message is also given to the Prophet Zechariah, who states:

"'And it shall come to pass

'*That* as you were a curse among the heathen,

'O house of Judah and house of Israel,

'So will I save you, and you shall be a blessing.

'Fear not,

'*But* let your hands be strong.'

For thus says the LORD of hosts:

'As I thought to punish you,

'When your fathers provoked me to wrath,'

Says the LORD of hosts,

'And I repented not,

'So again have I thought in these days

'To do well unto Jerusalem and to the house of Judah.

'Fear you not.'"

(Zechariah 8:13–15)

Despite all of the evidence from Scripture, there are many who teach that Armageddon does not include a literal gathering of military forces to battle against the Jews in Jerusalem. Perhaps the most vocal of these groups is the Seventh Day Adventist Church, which teaches many false interpretations of the end times events. In 1844, the SDA suffered its Great Disappointment when the anticipated Second Coming of Christ failed to materialise. Instead of accepting that they had made a mistake, the doctrine of "Investigative Judgement" was invented to avoid admitting that they got the date wrong. As we shall soon see, the Adventists are also completely misguided when it comes to the thousand years that follow Armageddon.

Zechariah continued his account of the great day of battle by stating:

"Behold, I will make Jerusalem a cup of trembling unto all the people round about, when they shall be in the siege both against Judah and against Jerusalem."

"And it shall come to pass in that day, *that* I will seek to destroy all the nations that come against Jerusalem."

(Zechariah 12:2, 9)

When the sixth angel pours out his vial upon the great river Euphrates, the waters are dried up to prepare the way for the kings of the east and their armies to come against Jerusalem. The Euphrates river forms a natural barrier that stretches from Syria's border with Turkey all the way to the Persian Gulf. Without it, there would be no obstacle in the way of a land invasion from Iran, Afghanistan, Pakistan, China or Russia.

Armageddon represents the final judgement upon the Earth, but it is far more than a battle against Jerusalem only. When the seventh angel pours out his vial, there is a great earthquake unlike anything that has been experienced since man has been upon the Earth. The cities of the nations fall, and great Babylon comes in remembrance before God, to receive the cup of the wine of the fierceness of His wrath. The great city, which refers to Rome, is divided in three, and during this time, a great hail falls from heaven, with men blaspheming God due to the plague of enormous hailstones

(Revelation 16:17–21).

Rome was the persecuting power during Christ's life and also during the time that John received the Revelation. When the Roman Empire accepted that Christianity could not be defeated, it realised that its survival was dependent upon controlling this potentially mortal threat to its authority. In 476 AD, the Western Roman Empire appeared to fall, but the Bishop of Rome, who would later become Pope, filled the power vacuum left by the Caesars, enabling the fourth beast kingdom to survive (to this day) after its deadly wound was healed.

Revelation 13 describes this transition, as Pagan Rome morphed into "what appeared to be Christian Rome", from the time of Emperor Constantine until the head wound of 476 AD. This phase of the Roman fourth beast is referred to as the beast out of the sea or as Revelation 17 describes it: the king who "is not yet come; and when he comes, he must continue a short space." Immediately following this, we see the rise of the beast out of the Earth – the Papacy – which heals the head wound, speaks great things against the Most High, appears lamblike but speaks as a Dragon, and makes war with the Saints and overcomes them. Revelation 17 describes this man as the eighth king who was also the beast that was, and is not, a reference to Babylon, which also appeared to fall but was resurrected by the Man of Sin who continued and established its Pagan worship throughout the world under the veil of Christianity.

"And he exercised all the power of the first beast before him, and caused the earth and them which dwell therein to worship the first beast, whose deadly wound was healed."

(Revelation 13:12)

The Prophet Daniel spoke of Mystery, Babylon the Great, the Papal earth beast as the "Little Horn" that rises amongst the ten horns on the head of the fourth beast, just as the Papacy emerged out of the ten divided nations of the Western Empire to take control of, and ride, the scarlet beast of Rome.

John is shown a vision of the judgement of the Great Whore in Revelation 17, which also includes a detailed description that leaves us in no doubt as to her identity. John is carried away in the spirit and sees a woman sitting upon a scarlet-coloured beast with seven heads and ten horns. Revelation 12 and 13 clearly identify this beast as Rome, the fourth kingdom, which incorporated features of the kingdoms that preceded it, as described in Daniel's 2nd chapter. The beast was like a leopard (Greece) with the feet of a bear (Medo-Persia) and the mouth of a lion (Babylon); the Woman riding the beast is also clearly identified.

"The woman was arrayed in purple and scarlet colour, and decked with gold and precious stones and pearls, having a golden cup in her hand, full of abominations and filthiness of her fornication.

And upon her forehead was a name written:
MYSTERY,
BABYLON THE GREAT,
THE MOTHER OF HARLOTS AND ABOMINATIONS OF THE EARTH.
And I saw the woman, drunken with the blood of the saints and with the blood of the martyrs of Jesus."

(Revelation 17:4–6)

Revelation 12 also describes the Church of Christ as a Woman, who had to flee into the wilderness to escape persecution after Satan was cast out of heaven, following Christ's ascension to sit at the right hand of God.

The Woman of Revelation 17 is also a church, but a false one that is under the direct influence of Satan to lead its followers away from Christ through false doctrine. The Roman Catholic Church has its cardinals and bishops arrayed in scarlet and purple, and they hold the golden communion cup of abominations that plays a key role in the continual sacrifice of the Eucharist. Over the past 1500 years, she has become drunk on power after shedding the blood of millions of Christian martyrs, who died rather than deny the true gospel and bow down to Satan's anointed one, the Pope of Rome, the Great Whore and Mother of Harlots that sits upon many waters.

Revelation 17 ends with John being told that the woman he saw is that great city, which reigns over the kings of the Earth. Vatican City, in the heart of Rome, is the seat of the Antichrist, where the Woman sits upon the seven mountains, as witnessed by John in Revelation 17:9.

The Roman Catholic Church is the world's largest Christian denomination, with approximately two billion followers. The Pope is seen by them as Christ's vicar on Earth, and as such, he has tremendous power and influence, to the extent that Catholics will follow his dictates over those of their countries' leaders. This power is well known by all governments, kings and world leaders, who have to stay in favour with the Vatican in order to survive. The Pope can decide elections and overthrow governments due to the enormous influence he holds, which is why the church he controls was seen by John as a whore that sits upon many waters and reigns over the kings of the Earth.

The monumental sins and evil of the Synagogue of Satan have reached up to heaven, and God has remembered her iniquities, with Revelation 18 describing her destruction during the pouring out of the seventh vial. The events that occur during this final plague mark God's "great reset", as opposed to Satan's counterfeit, which we hear so much about today. The World Economic Forum's "great reset" is nothing more than the New World Order, which is Satan's final attempt to restructure the Earth to follow his values and destroy faith in the one true God.

"How much she has glorified herself and lived deliciously, so much torment and sorrow give her; for she says in her heart, 'I sit a queen, and am no widow, and shall see no sorrow.'

Therefore shall her plagues come in one day; death, and mourning, and famine. And she shall be utterly burnt with fire, for strong is the LORD God, who judges her."

(Revelation 18:7–8)

This decree by God was foretold centuries before when Isaiah stated:

"Therefore hear now this, *you that are* given to pleasures,

That dwells carelessly,

That says in your heart,

'I *am*, and none else besides me;

'I shall not sit *as* a widow,

'Neither shall I know the loss of children.'

But these two *things* shall come to you

In a moment, in one day:

The loss of children, and widowhood;

They shall come upon you in their perfection

For the multitude of your sorceries,

And for the great abundance of your enchantments.

For you have trusted in your wickedness;
You have said, 'None sees me.'
Your wisdom and your knowledge, it has perverted you,
And you have said in your heart,
'I *am*, and none else besides me.'
Therefore shall evil come upon you;
You shall not know from where it rises.
And mischief shall fall upon you;
You shall not be able to put it off.
And desolation shall come upon you suddenly,
Which you shall not know.
Stand now with your enchantments
And with the multitude of your sorceries,
Wherein you have laboured from your youth;
If so be you shall be able to profit,
If so be you may prevail.
You are wearied in the multitude of your counsels;
Let now the astrologers, the stargazers,
The monthly prognosticators
Stand up and save you
From *these things* that shall come upon you.
Behold, they shall be as stubble,
The fire shall burn them;
They shall not deliver themselves
From the power of the flame;
There shall not be a coal to warm at,
Nor fire to sit before it!
Thus shall they be unto you
With whom you have laboured,
Even your merchants from your youth;

They shall wander every one to his quarter.

None shall save you."

(Isaiah 47:8–15)

The Prophet Zephaniah also spoke of the destruction of the Papal Antichrist's kingdom when he stated:

"This *is* the rejoicing city

That dwelt carelessly,

That said in her heart,

'I *am*, and *there is* none beside me.'

How is she become a desolation,

A place for beasts to lie down in!

Every one that passes by her

Shall hiss *and* wag his hand."

(Zephaniah 2:15)

Revelation 18 gives many details and potential clues regarding the destruction of Mystery, Babylon the Great, which will mark an end to Satan's influence over the kingdoms of Earth. We are told that her plagues will come in one day, that she will be utterly burnt with fire. The kings of the Earth shall lament for her when they see the smoke of her burning, standing afar off for fear of her torment.

Saying alas, alas, that great city Babylon, that mighty city: for in one hour is your judgement come.

The merchants of the earth shall stand afar off for fear of her torment saying alas, alas, that great city that was clothed in fine linen, and purple, and scarlet, and decked with gold, and precious stones, and pearls:

For in one hour so great riches is come to nought.

Every shipmaster, and as many as trade by sea stood afar off and cried when they saw the smoke of her burning, saying, what city is like unto this great city?

And they cast dust on their heads, and cried, weeping and wailing saying alas, alas, that great city, wherein were made rich all that had ships in the sea by reason of her costliness, for in one hour is she made desolate.

Rejoice over her, you heaven, and you holy apostles and Prophets, for God has avenged you on her.

And a mighty angel took up a stone like a great millstone, and cast it into the sea, saying, thus with violence shall that great city Babylon be thrown down, and shall be found no more at all.

The chapter ends by saying:

"for by your sorceries were all nations deceived.

And in her was found the blood of prophets and of saints, and of all that were slain upon the earth."

When I first read Revelation 18's description of the destructive judgement upon Mystery, Babylon, I was immediately reminded of another event, of similar magnitude, that had happened in the past. In 79AD, only nine years after Jerusalem and its temple had been destroyed by Titus and his 10th Legion, Mount Vesuvius, which was only 125 miles from the centre of Rome, erupted, famously burying the wealthy city of Pompeii. Everything described in this chapter of Revelation seems to be a perfect match for a huge volcanic eruption, and Vesuvius may well have been a foreshadowing of Rome's ultimate fate!

God warned that sudden destruction would come upon her, with her plagues coming in one day and that she should be utterly burnt with fire. The description of kings and merchants standing afar off for fear of her torment and burning would perfectly describe those watching a city being destroyed by a volcanic eruption. Casting dust upon their heads, crying and weeping, would also fit this scenario, as would the angel casting a great stone into the sea "saying, 'Thus with violence shall that great city Babylon be thrown down, and shall be found no more at all.'"

Daniel prophesied that the final kingdom upon Earth would be struck by a stone, cut out without hands, bringing an end to all the earthly kingdoms. This stone that struck the great image upon the feet in King Nebuchadnezzar's dream not only stood for the level of devastation that the fourth beast would suffer, but also symbolised Christ, who would return to put an end to the Antichrist's kingdom and set up His own, which would become a mountain that filled the whole Earth.

Daniel went on to describe the rise of the fourth beast kingdom of Rome, foretelling how it would stand up against the Prince of Princes but that it shall be broken without hand (Daniel 8:25). The breaking "without hand" seems to imply that Rome's destruction will not come from a human adversary but, rather, by an act of God Himself. Again, this would perfectly describe a Vesuvius-like event, as would the events we see following the pouring out of the seventh vial at the end of Revelation 16.

The seventh vial brings God's final judgement upon the wicked nations of Earth who have refused to obey His commandments and denied His Son. We are told how there will be:

"[...] a great earthquake, such as was not since men were upon the earth, so mighty an earthquake, *and* so great.

And the great city was divided into three parts, and the cities of the nations fell; and great Babylon came in remembrance before God, to give unto her the cup of the wine of the fierceness of his wrath."

"And there fell upon men a great hail out of heaven, *every stone* about the weight of a talent, and men blasphemed God because of the plague of the hail, for the plague thereof was exceeding great."

(Revelation 16:18–19, 21)

All of these things are consistent with a huge volcanic eruption, so I started wondering if there is a volcano close enough to Rome to cause this devastation. Again, a simple online search revealed the fact that such a volcano does indeed exist less than 15 miles southeast of Rome's centre in the Alban Hills, visible from the Vatican.

Scientists believed that the Colli Albani was an extinct volcano, but in 2016, the news reported that it was showing signs of new activity. These reports followed the 6.2 magnitude earthquake that hit approximately sixty-five miles northeast of Rome in August of that year. One headline read, "Sleeping volcano to wipe out Rome: Italy earthquake could trigger BIBLICAL eruption". Researchers were saying that massive earthquakes can bring sleeping volcanoes back to life, and that Colli Albani has the potential to be more explosive than Mount Vesuvius![1]

Revelation 19 describes the final events of Armageddon and the destruction brought about by the pouring out of the seventh vial. The beast and the false prophet being taken and cast alive into a lake of fire burning with brimstone may well describe the poetic justice that befalls the Woman and the beast that she rides. God knows the end from the beginning, so it's entirely possible that He buried a sleeping giant beneath Satan's final kingdom that would be ready to utterly devour her at the appointed time. The great earthquake that divides the city into three could submerge Rome and the Vatican into a lake of fire, as foreseen in Jeremiah 51:64:

"Thus shall Babylon sink, and shall not rise from the evil that I will bring upon her."

Armageddon marks God's final judgement upon the current age, from Creation in Eden to Christ's return. How this great battle is fought cannot be known for sure; Scripture only tells us that the kings of the Earth and their armies will be gathered together to make war against Christ and His army, but the details are missing. There are clues, however, but as with all events that are yet in the future, we can only speculate within the bounds of what has been written.

Following the destruction of Mystery, Babylon, Revelation 19 begins by stating:

"And after these things I heard a great voice of much people in heaven, saying, 'Alleluia! Salvation, and glory, and honour, and power unto the LORD our God!

'For true and righteous are His judgements, for He has judged the great whore which did corrupt the earth with her fornication, and has avenged the blood of His servants at her hand.'

And again they said, 'Alleluia! And her smoke rose up for ever and ever.'" (1–3)

When the angel cried mightily with a strong voice saying, "Babylon the great is fallen, is fallen", he was acknowledging that both literal Babylon and now its revived spiritual twin (the church/state system of Papal Rome) had been destroyed.

"Behold, the day of the LORD comes,

Cruel both with wrath and fierce anger,

To lay the land desolate;

And he shall destroy the sinners thereof out of it.

For the stars of heaven, and the constellations thereof

Shall not give their light;

The sun shall be darkened in his going forth,

And the moon shall not cause her light to shine.

And I will punish the world for *their* evil,

And the wicked for their iniquity;

And I will cause the arrogancy of the proud to cease,

And will lay low the haughtiness of the terrible."

"Therefore I will shake the heavens,

And the earth shall remove out of her place,

In the wrath of the LORD of Hosts

And in the day of his fierce anger."

"And Babylon, the glory of kingdoms,

The beauty of the Chaldees' excellency,

Shall be as when God overthrew Sodom and Gomorrah."

(Isaiah 13:9–11, 13, 19)

The great throne room in heaven witnesses that the marriage of the Lamb is come, and His wife (the Church) has made herself ready. And to her was granted that she should be arrayed in fine linen, clean and white, for the fine linen is the righteousness of Saints.

John watches as heaven is opened and he beholds a white horse, and He that sat upon him was called faithful and true, and in righteousness He does judge and make war. The description of Christ is clear, and the armies which were in heaven followed Him upon white horses, clothed in fine linen, white and clean, ready to meet the armies that were gathered against them in the valley of decision.

Whether there will be an actual, physical battle between them is not recorded, and we can only wonder how a mortal army could wage war with conventional weapons against an immortal, heavenly army. We are told that out of Christ's mouth will go a sharp, two-edged sword with which He should smite the nations and slay their remnant, and that He treads the winepress of the fierceness and wrath of Almighty God. Hebrews 4:12 tells us that the Word of God is quick and powerful, and sharper than any two-edged sword, which could imply that Christ would be defeating the remnant of nations with the great truth He will speak – the sword that proceeds from His mouth.

The actual destruction of the beast's army may come directly from God via the great earthquake and the hail that rains down from heaven:

"'but the same day that Lot went out of Sodom it rained fire and brimstone from heaven and destroyed them all;

Even thus shall it be in the day when the Son of man is revealed.'"

(Luke 17:29–30)

"For the indignation of the LORD is upon all nations,
And his fury upon all their armies;
He has utterly destroyed them,
He has delivered them to the slaughter."

(Isaiah 34:2)

Jesus "treading the winepress of the wrath of Almighty God" could represent Christ setting up his millennial reign upon the smouldering remains of Satan's kingdom, after he is bound with a great chain by the angel and cast into the bottomless pit for **1000** years, that he should deceive the nations no more till the **1000** years should be fulfilled.

"You have defiled your sanctuaries

By the multitude of your iniquities,

By the iniquity of your trade;

Therefore will I bring forth a fire from the midst of you,

It shall devour you,

And I will bring you to ashes upon the earth

In the sight of all them that behold you."

(Ezekiel 28:18)

Further confirmation that this may be the case is recorded in the final chapter of the Old Testament that states:

"'For behold, the day comes,

'That shall burn as an oven,

'And all the proud, yea, and all that do wickedly shall be stubble;

'And the day that comes shall burn them up,'

Says the LORD of hosts,

'That it shall leave them neither root nor branch.

'But unto you that fear my name

'Shall the Sun of Righteousness arise

'With healing in his wings,

'And shall go forth

'And grow up as calves of the stall.

'And you shall tread down the wicked,

'For they shall be ashes under the soles of your feet

'In the day that I shall do this,'

Says the LORD of hosts."

(Malachi 4:1–3)

1   'Sleeping volcano to wipe out Rome', Article by Joshua Nevett, Daily Star UK. 25th August 2016.

    'Volcano on Rome's doorstep is slowly reawakening', Article by Benjamin Kentish, The Independent UK. 1st November 2016.

    'Dormant Volcano Poised to destroy Rome in 1000 years', Article by Kristina Killgrove, Forbes.com. 13th July 2016.

CHAPTER XV

THE MILLENNIAL REIGN

When the Jews' Messiah came, He was rejected by them for many reasons. Jesus arrived at a time of great turmoil for Israel; their holy city and temple were under the control of the Roman Empire, and many were crying out for Messiah to come to deliver them from the oppression of Rome.

Jesus was not accepted by the majority of Jews as, in their eyes, the prophesied Messiah was supposed to regather Israel, bring them back into the land and rebuild the temple. Obviously, this couldn't happen as the Jews were already in the land and the temple was still standing; so, why did Jesus show up when He did?

Sadly, the Jews concentrated on the prophecies concerning Messiah coming to deliver them and end their suffering, but overlooked the fact that the Prophets had foretold that He would first be rejected by them.

"The stone which the builders refused

Is become the head of the corner."

(Psalms 118:22)

All of the suffering that would befall the Jewish nation was a result of them not listening to God when He constantly warned them of the consequences of their disobedience. The Jews are still anxiously awaiting the arrival of Messiah, without realising that it will be His Second Coming; the 2300 years of suffering that they will have endured by the time He returns are a direct result of His rejection and execution in 30AD.

"'Awake, O sword, against my shepherd,

'And against the man *that is* my fellow,'

Says the LORD of hosts.

'Smite the shepherd,

'And the sheep shall be scattered;

'And I will turn my hand upon the little ones.'"

(Zechariah 13:7)

Jesus arrived in Jerusalem on the back of a donkey on the 10th day of the first month, the day Scripture tells us that the Passover lamb was to be chosen.

"Rejoice greatly, O daughter of Zion!

Shout, O daughter of Jerusalem!

Behold, your King comes unto you;

He *is* just, and having salvation,

Lowly, and riding upon an ass,

And upon a colt, the foal of an ass."

(Zechariah 9:9)

All the signs were there that Messiah had come, but the eyes of the Jews were blinded to the point that they turned on Him and delivered Him up to be killed at the same time that the Passover lambs were being sacrificed, fulfilling God's promise to Abraham that He would provide the lamb.

Christ's suffering and death was foretold in great detail by the Prophets, and spoken of in the Psalms.

"He trusted on the LORD, that he would deliver him;

Let him deliver him, seeing he delighted in him."

(Psalms 22:8)

Mathew's gospel tells how the chief priests, scribes and elders mocked Jesus, saying:

"'He trusted in God; let Him deliver Him now if He will have Him; for He said, "I am the Son of God."'"

(Matthew 27:43)

"For dogs have compassed me;

The assembly of the wicked have enclosed me.

They pierced my hands and my feet;

I may tell all my bones.

They look and stare upon me.

They part my garments among them,

And cast lots upon my vesture."

(Psalms 22:16–18)

This wasn't the only Psalm that spoke clearly of Messiah's suffering and death upon the Cross. Psalm 69 states:

"I am weary of my crying,

My throat is dried:

My eyes fail while I wait for my God.

They that hate me without a cause,

Are more than the hairs of my head;

They that would destroy me, being my enemies wrongfully, are mighty;

Then I restored that which I took not away."

"Reproach has broken my heart,

And I am full of heaviness;

And I looked for some to take pity, but there was none;

And for comforters, but I found none.

They gave me also gall for my meat,

And in my thirst they gave me vinegar to drink."

(Psalm 69:3–4, 20–21)

These prophetic words precisely correspond with the gospel accounts of the Crucifixion of Jesus in every detail, but Isaiah's 53rd chapter leaves us in no doubt:

"Who has believed our report?

And to whom is the arm of the LORD revealed?

For he shall grow up before him as a tender plant,

And as a root out of a dry ground.

He has no form nor comeliness;

And when we shall see him,

There is no beauty that we should desire him.

He is despised and rejected of men,

A man of sorrows, and acquainted with grief.

And we hid, as it were, our faces from him;

He was despised, and we esteemed him not.

Surely he has bourn our griefs

And carried our sorrows;

Yet we did esteem him stricken,

Smitten of God, and afflicted.

But he was wounded for our transgressions,

He was bruised for our iniquities;

The chastisement of our peace was upon him,

And with his stripes we are healed.

All we like sheep have gone astray;

We have turned, every one, to his own way,

And the LORD has laid on him the iniquity of us all.

He was oppressed and he was afflicted,

Yet he opened not his mouth;

He is brought as a lamb to the slaughter,

And as a sheep before her shearers is dumb,

So he opened not his mouth.

He was taken from prison and from judgment,

And who shall declare his generation?

For he was cut off out of the land of the living,

For the transgression of my people was he stricken.

And he made his grave with the wicked,

And with the rich in his death,

Because he had done no violence,

Neither was any deceit in his mouth.

Yet it pleased the LORD to bruise him,

He has put him to grief.

When you shall make his soul an offering for sin,

He shall see his seed, he shall prolong his days,

And the pleasure of the LORD shall prosper in his hand.

He shall see of the travail of his soul, and shall be satisfied.

By his knowledge shall my righteous servant justify many,

For he shall bear their iniquities.

Therefore will I divide him a portion with the great,

And he shall divide the spoil with the strong,

Because he has poured out his soul unto death,

And he was numbered with the transgressors,

And he bore the sins of many,

And made intercession for the transgressors."

The strong military leader that the Jews were expecting never materialised; instead, they were faced with an ordinary-looking man who came preaching a message of peace.

Disobedience to God's laws had brought about all the wickedness and sin in the world, and Jesus was sent to teach that their hearts needed to change before a millennium of peace could exist. The Jews were not ready for the message that they should love their enemies, so their Messiah was rejected and killed, just as the Prophets had foretold.

Gabriel's warning to Daniel, that his people were to be given 70 weeks of years to end the transgression and bring in everlasting righteousness, was coming to an end. Only three and a half years remained for the Jews to accept their mistake, and if they had succeeded, the millennial reign of Christ would have started there and then, without the need for the 2300 years of desolation that followed. God knows the end from the beginning, so their failure to accept Messiah at that time allowed God to plan for the salvation of the Gentiles, who could now obtain the free gift of grace through faith after hearing the gospel that came first to the Jews.

Despite the Jews' failure to end the transgression, the indignation would be limited to the time decreed, before God would once again remember His covenant with Abraham, Isaac and Jacob, and a remnant of Israel would be saved.

"For thus says the LORD God, 'Behold, I, even I will both search My sheep, and seek them out.

'As a shepherd seeks out his flock in the day that he is among his sheep that are scattered, so will I seek out My sheep and will deliver them out of all places where they have been scattered in the cloudy and dark day.

'And I will bring them out from the peoples, and gather them from the countries, and will bring them to their own land, and feed them upon the mountains of Israel by the rivers, and in all the inhabited places of the country.'"

(Ezekiel 34:11–13)

Isaiah spoke of the fact that God's people were being led astray by those entrusted to guide them:

"For the leaders of this people cause them to err,

And they that are led of them, are destroyed."

(Isaiah 9:16)

The Prophet Ezekiel warned them, saying:

"therefore, O you shepherds, hear the word of the LORD!

Thus says the LORD God, 'Behold, I am against the shepherds, and I will require my flock at their hand, and cause them to cease from feeding the flock, neither shall the shepherds feed themselves anymore; for I will deliver my flock from their mouth, that they may not be meat for them.'"

(Ezekiel 34:9–10)

Armageddon, the great and terrible day of the LORD, the cloudy and dark day, will bring about the destruction of both the wicked nations that opposed God and His Christ, and also the Jewish leaders who caused God's people to become lost.

"Zion shall be redeemed with judgement,

And her converts with righteousness.

And the destruction of the transgressors and of the sinners shall be together,

And they that forsake the LORD shall be consumed."

(Isaiah 1:27–28)

Many of the Prophets spoke of the day of the LORD, saying how it would be a day of darkness and not light, a day of gloominess, of clouds and thick darkness, but that when God had finished His work to purge the Earth of evil, all that will change as He ushers in the millennial age.

"Moreover the light of the moon shall be as the light of the sun,

And the light of the sun shall be sevenfold,

As the light of seven days,

In the day that the LORD binds up the breach of his people,

And heals the stroke of their wound."

(Isaiah 30:26)

This is confirmed by Zechariah, who wrote:

"But it shall be one day,

Which shall be known to the LORD,

Not day nor night;

But it shall come to pass that at evening time

It shall be light."

(Zechariah 14:7)

When Christ returns and all eyes see Him together with the Saints, arriving on the clouds of heaven with power and great glory, there shall be a great mourning in Jerusalem.

"And I will pour upon the house of David, and upon the inhabitants of Jerusalem, the spirit of grace and of supplications; and they shall look upon me whom they have pierced. And they shall mourn for him, as one mourns for his only son, and shall be in bitterness for him, as one that is in bitterness for his firstborn."

(Zechariah 12:10)

This remnant was often spoken of by the Prophets, with Isaiah stating:

"And it shall come to pass in that day,

That the remnant of Israel,

And such as are escaped of the house of Jacob,

Shall no more again stay upon him that smote them;

But shall stay upon the LORD, the Holy One of Israel, in truth.

The remnant shall return, even the remnant of Jacob,

Unto the Mighty God.

For though your people, Israel, be as the sand of the sea,

Yet a remnant of them shall return;

The consumption decreed shall overflow with righteousness."

(Isaiah 10:20–22)

Jeremiah also told how God would gather the remnant of His flock out of all the countries that He had driven them to, and Amos spoke of God sifting the house of Israel among all nations, to bring again the captivity of His people after the sinners amongst them were to die by the sword. When the Jews started returning to the land, following the formation of the nation state of Israel in 1948, this was seen by many as a fulfilment of Biblical prophecy, despite the fact that Scripture describes this event as occurring *after* the cataclysmic events of Armageddon. The remnant that God will bring back into the land will be those who turn from transgression and seek after His ways, rather than the false regathering that was brought about by those

"That say, 'Let him make a speed, and hasten his work,

'That we may see it;

'And let the counsel of the Holy One of Israel draw nigh and come,

'That we may know it!'"

(Isaiah 5:19)

When God heals the rift with His people that was caused by their failure to end the transgression in 33 AD, it will be a new beginning marked by many incredible events to welcome the millennial reign of His Son upon the Earth. The great day of God's judgement that was filled with darkness will end with the moon shining as brightly as the sun. God's people will witness Christ coming in the clouds, together with the Saints, and they will be in mourning when they look upon Him whom they pierced and realise that their people indeed rejected and killed their own Messiah over 2000 years before. The Mount of Olives shall cleave in two when He sets foot upon it, forming a great valley, and it shall be in that day that living waters shall go out from Jerusalem, and there shall be no more utter destruction, but Jerusalem shall be safely inhabited.

The long-awaited time of peace and safety for the Jewish nation, that they were hoping for in 30 AD, will finally arrive, and God will pour upon the house of David, and upon the inhabitants of Jerusalem, the spirit of grace and of supplications.

"And it shall come to pass in the last days
That the mountain of the LORD's house
Shall be established in the top of the mountains,
And shall be exalted above the hills;
And all nations shall flow into it."

(Isaiah 2:2)

This is the great temple, the house of the LORD that was spoken of by the Prophet Ezekiel and others, where the LORD will:

"dwell in the midst of Jerusalem,

And Jerusalem shall be called a city of truth,

And the mountain of the LORD of hosts, the Holy Mountain."

(Zechariah 8:3)

Ezekiel spoke in great detail about the millennial temple in the 40th to 47th chapters of his book. Many people believe that this wasn't a literal prophecy, but there is overwhelming evidence throughout the Bible to say otherwise. Virtually all of the Prophets spoke of the time when Israel would live in peace in their own land and how it would be the Messiah who would reign during this golden age. The founding of the nation state of Israel in 1948 bears no resemblance to the age spoken of by the Prophets, where the city would have no need to be walled and the inhabitants would live without fear. Ever since its founding, there has been constant unrest in Israel, with enemies on all sides who want to see it destroyed; this more closely resembles the build-up to Armageddon than the millennium of peace!

Contrast the above with God's description of how Israel shall live:

"And they shall no more be a prey to the heathen, neither shall the beasts of the land devour them; but they shall dwell safely, and none shall make them afraid."
(Ezekiel 34:28. See also: Zephaniah 3:13, Job 11:19, Jeremiah 46:27 & Leviticus 26:6)

During this time, Israel will live in peace and safety, but it will also be a time of reflection as they relearn the things God tried to teach them in the past, thereby making amends for their transgressions and iniquity.

"'Fear you not, O Jacob, my servant,' says the LORD,
'For I am with you;

'For I will make a full end of all the nations

'Where I have driven you,

'But I will not make a full end of you,

'But correct you in measure,

'Yet will I not leave you wholly unpunished.'"

(Jeremiah 46:28)

"'Then shall you remember your own evil ways, and your doings that were not good, and shall loathe yourselves in your own sight for your iniquities and for your abominations.

'Not for your sakes do I this,' says the LORD God, 'be it known unto you; be ashamed and confounded for your own ways, O house of Israel!'"

(Ezekiel 36:31–32)

During the millennium, Jesus will reign from the temple that shall be rebuilt to far exceed those that preceded it and a sacrificial system will be reintroduced at the temple – and this is where many Christians feel very conflicted. The gospels tell us that Christ was the final sacrifice acceptable to God, that it was His death that paid the price for sin.

The sacrificial system was a schoolmaster that pointed to Christ, it was instituted to teach us that we are incapable of paying the price for our own salvation and that we would have to trust in another who would be acceptable to God. Christ's sacrifice, after living a perfect, sinless life of obedience, fulfilled God's requirement for a lamb without mark or blemish. We, too, could now be covered by His righteousness in God's eyes and receive the free gift of grace through faith in the One who paid the price for us. This incredible gift is open to all those who put their faith in Jesus prior to his return, where they will live and reign with Him during the 1000 years of peace on Earth.

The new sacrificial system in the millennial kingdom will be more of a memorial, to teach the Jews the original purpose of the sacrifice so they can bear their shame.

"Wash me thoroughly from my iniquity,

And cleanse me from my sin.

For I acknowledge my transgressions, and my sin is ever before me."

"Create in me a clean heart, O God,

And renew a right spirit within me."

"Then will I teach transgressors your ways,

And sinners shall be converted unto you."

"The sacrifices of God are a broken spirit;

A broken and a contrite heart,

O God, you will not despise.

Do good in your good pleasure unto Zion;

Build you the walls of Jerusalem.

Then shall you be pleased with the sacrifices of righteousness,

With burnt offering;

Then shall they offer bullocks upon your altar."

(Psalm 51:2–3, 10, 13, 17–19)

"'And when these days are expired, it shall be that upon the eighth day and so forward, the priests shall make your burnt offerings upon the altar, and your peace offerings; and I will accept you,' says the LORD God."

(Ezekiel 43:27)

The millennial reign will be a time of peace and learning where the world will be exposed to the truth of who God is, when His Messiah will instruct them in His ways from God's Holy Mountain.

"And many people shall go and say,

'Come you and let us go up to the mountain of the LORD,

To the house of the God of Jacob,

And he will teach us of his ways,

And we will walk in his paths.'

For out of Zion shall go forth the law,

And the word of the LORD from Jerusalem."

(Isaiah 2:3)

"They shall not hurt nor destroy in all my Holy Mountain,

For the earth shall be full of knowledge of the LORD,

As the waters cover the sea."

(Isaiah 11:9)

Everything you have just read indicates a clear narrative throughout Scripture that God would save a remnant of His people to live at peace in their own land, under the rule of their Messiah, for 1000 years. Despite all the evidence, many people believe that the millennial reign of Christ will not be on Earth at all, but in heaven.

The main proponents of this false teaching are the Seventh Day Adventists, who are also responsible for many other false doctrines, as outlined in previous chapters. The SDA not only teaches that there will not be a physical battle over Jerusalem during Armageddon, they also say that Satan being cast into the bottomless pit for 1000 years actually refers to him (and the angels that followed him) being left alone on Earth, which will be uninhabited.[1] They teach that everyone on Earth will be killed apart from the Saints, who will be in heaven with Christ, overseeing the evidence of God's judgement upon those who were not part of the first resurrection.[2] Following the 1000 years, the dead will

be resurrected, and Satan will be free to deceive them once
more; New Jerusalem will descend out of heaven, and Satan,
together with his army, will come against it, only to be destroyed by God's wrath.[3]

Unfortunately, this version of events sounds quite plausible, and millions of people blindly follow the teachings of
hugely popular preachers, such as Doug Batchelor, Professor Walter Veith and Steve Wohlberg, without diligently
studying the scriptures for themselves.

Because the SDA is so prominent when it comes to the
prophetic events of the end times, it is important to break
down their claims, and show them to be false due to their
placing of verses in the wrong order and context. First of all,
we will address their assertion that all life on Earth will end
and only Satan and his angels will remain for 1000 years.
Jeremiah chapter 4 is used as evidence for this when it states:

"I beheld the earth, and it was without form, and void;
And the heavens, they had no light."
"I beheld, and there was no man,
And all the birds of the heavens were fled.
I beheld, and the fruitful place was a wilderness,
And all the cities thereof were broken down
At the presence of the LORD,
And by his fierce anger."

(Jeremiah 4:23, 25–26)

When you cherry-pick verses like these and take them
out of context, it results in the casual listener being moulded
to follow whatever doctrine is being pushed. The subject of
these final chapters relates to Israel's disobedience and the
prophetic warnings of the consequences they would face if

they continued in their wickedness. The descriptions of devastation refer to the aftermath of Armageddon, that dark and terrible day of destruction against the nations that oppose God. The verses quoted by the SDA are deliberately cut short to omit the following:

"For thus has the LORD said:

'The whole land shall be desolate;

'Yet will I not make a full end.'"

(Jeremiah 4:27)

The next chapter repeats this twice with Jeremiah 5:10, 18 stating:

"Go you up upon her walls, and destroy,

But make not a full end;

Take away her battlements,

For they are not the LORD's."

"'Nevertheless in those days,' says the LORD, 'I will not make a full end with you.'"

These statements are conveniently overlooked by the SDA, as they back up the fact that a remnant of Israel will be saved to return to Jerusalem and live in peace as God had promised.

Another favourite verse that is used by the Adventists to back up their view that there will be nobody left on Earth is Jeremiah 25:33, which states:

"And the slain of the LORD shall be at that day from one end of the earth even unto the other end of the earth; they shall not be lamented, neither gathered nor buried; they shall be dung upon the ground."

The claim is that they will not be buried because there will be nobody left on Earth to bury them, but the Prophet

Zephaniah used the same language in reference to the battle of Armageddon when he said:

"That day is a day of wrath,

A day of trouble and distress,

A day of wasteness and desolation,

A day of darkness and gloominess,

A day of clouds and thick darkness,"

"And I will bring distress upon men,

That they shall walk like blind men,

Because they have sinned against the LORD,

And their blood shall be poured out as dust,

And their flesh as the dung."

(Zephaniah 1:15, 17)

These bodies will not be buried because they will be given to the fowls that fly in the midst of heaven when the angel calls them to gather themselves together unto the supper of the great God, to eat the flesh of kings, captains and mighty men (Revelation 19:17–18).

If any doubts remain as to whether the Earth will be inhabited during the millennial reign, these are dispelled by Zechariah, who states:

"And it shall come to pass that everyone that is left of all the nations which came against Jerusalem shall even go up from year to year to worship the King, the LORD of hosts, and to keep the Feast of Tabernacles.

And it shall be, that who so will not come up of all the families of the earth unto Jerusalem, to worship the King, the LORD of hosts, even upon them shall be no rain."

(Zechariah 14:16–17)

These are the people that Christ and the Saints will reign over during the 1000 years that follow Armageddon, and the disobedient amongst them will be the ones who will be readily deceived by Satan when he is released from his prison.

During the millennium, Zechariah tells us that:

"In that day there shall be a fountain opened to the house of David and to the inhabitants of Jerusalem, for sin, and for uncleanness."

(Zechariah 13:1)

He goes on to say:

"That living waters shall go out from Jerusalem,

Half of them towards the former sea

And half of them towards the hinder sea."

(Zechariah 14:8)

The Prophet Ezekiel also described these living, or healing, waters in his detailed account of the great temple that would be in Jerusalem when God has regathered His people:

"Afterward he brought me again unto the door of the house; and behold, waters issued out from under the threshold of the house eastward; for the forefront of the house stood toward the east, and the waters came down from under from the right side of the house, at the south side of the altar."

"Then said he unto me, 'These waters issue out toward the east country, and go down into the desert, and go into the sea; which being brought forth into the sea, the waters shall be healed.'"

(Ezekiel 47:1, 8)

It should be remembered that during the pouring out of the second vial judgement, as described in Revelation 16:3:

"The second angel poured out his vial upon the sea, and it became as the blood of a dead man; and every living soul died in the sea."

Armageddon occurs during the pouring of the sixth and seventh vials, with the millennial reign of Christ that follows returning life to the land for God's people to prosper.

We will talk more about these healing waters in the following chapter, as the false teachings of the Jesuit-influenced SDA will be exposed when we take a closer look at their doctrine regarding the Battle of Gog and Magog and the New Jerusalem.

1 & 2 White, Ellen G., *The Great Controversy Between Christ and Satan*, chapter 41: Desolation of the Earth. 1888. The International Tract Society Ltd., Watford, Herts, UK.

    In this chapter, White quotes Isaiah 24:6, saying:

    "Therefore has the curse devoured the earth, and they that dwell therein are desolate; therefore the inhabitants of the earth are burned."

    She conveniently omits the end of this verse which states:

    "And few men left."

    A deliberate deception!

3 White. Ellen G., *The Great Controversy Between Christ and Satan*, chapter 42: The Controversy Ended. 1888. The International Tract Society Ltd., Watford, Herts, UK.

CHAPTER XVI

GOG, MAGOG AND THE NEW JERUSALEM

The Gog and Magog war, which is spoken of in Ezekiel 38 and 39 and Revelation 20, is another part of the end times that is shrouded in mystery. Many people think that this prophecy is talking about Russia and link it to the current conflict between Russia and Ukraine, speculating that the troubles will expand, leading to Russia coming against Israel. Iran and Turkey are two countries that are also mentioned in regard to this prophetic battle, but Scripture doesn't tell us exactly who will be involved.

Ezekiel is told by God to prophesy against Gog, the land of Magog, the chief prince of Meshech and Tubal, and all his army: Persia, Ethiopia, Libya, Gomer, Togarmah of the north and all their bands and many people with him. God tells how, in the latter years, an evil thought will come into the mind of Gog, and together with his armies, he will come against Israel as a cloud to cover the land (Ezekiel 38).

It is futile to spend too much time speculating on who these nations will be because none of this occurs for at least 1500 years, and Revelation 20:8 makes it clear that Gog and

Magog represent the nations that are in the four quarters of the Earth who will be deceived and gathered by Satan to battle. The fact that people are linking current events to this battle shows how much deception there is concerning the end times, with the Gog/Magog war being placed in the wrong time period, just prior to Christ's return.

It can be quite difficult to place these events in the correct order because Armageddon and Gog and Magog are both described in similar terms and scattered throughout the writings of the Prophets. The book of Revelation is a great help here as it clearly lays out the timeline we are speaking of in a few short verses, but that doesn't stop false teachers from placing them in any order they choose to suit whatever doctrine they are pushing upon their audiences.

Taken in order of writing, Revelation 18 describes the destruction of Rome – the church/state system, the Woman that rides the beast, otherwise known as Mystery, Babylon the Great. This is followed in chapter 19 by Christ and His army returning to smite the nations that come against Him at Armageddon, and to set up His kingdom to rule over those who remain. Revelation 20 sees Satan being bound and cast into the bottomless pit for 1000 years, whilst Christ and the Saints, who are part of the first resurrection, live and reign on Earth during the new millennium.

When the 1000 years are expired, Satan is loosed from his prison to go out and deceive the nations of earth, Gog and Magog, to gather them together to do battle against Christ and the Saints. The Holy City Jerusalem and the camp of the Saints is surrounded, then God rains down fire from heaven to devour them, and Satan is cast into the lake of fire where the beast and the false prophet are, symbolising complete destruction.

Following this, we see the great white throne judgement, where all the dead, who were not part of the first resurrection, stand before God and are judged out of the books that were kept to record their works in life. Those who are not found to be worthy are also cast into the lake of fire, which is the permanent second death.

John then witnesses a new heaven and a new earth with:

"The Holy City, New Jerusalem, coming down from God out of heaven, prepared as a bride adorned for her husband."
(Revelation 21:1–2)

When you take the order of events given by God in his final revelation, you really can't go wrong, as those things spoken of by the Prophets have to fit into this timeline. Confusion often arises because many of the judgements spoken of by the Prophets have a dual fulfilment, with one occurring close to when the warning was given, but a greater fulfilment occurring at the end of days, if the lesson wasn't learnt.

We saw in the previous chapter how the SDA falsely teaches that there will be nobody living upon Earth during the millennial reign, apart from Satan and his angels. We will now examine their other claims.

The Adventists say that those who were not part of the first resurrection will come back to life following the millennium, only to appear back on Earth to be deceived by Satan once again.[1] This makes absolutely no sense for many reasons, as we shall see.

If the only people on Earth are those who were deceived in their previous life, then Satan will have no work to do as there will be nobody to bring them to Christ.

God wants us to make a conscious decision to choose Him and His Son over Satan, which is a major part of the purpose of the 1000-year reign of Christ upon the Earth. During this time, Jesus will rule from Jerusalem, together with the Saints, and the law will once again go out into the world, to those nations who survived the great purge of Armageddon.

After this time, Satan will be given his final opportunity to deceive the nations, who will be without excuse as the teachings of God and his Christ will be known by all. Satan is only to be given a relatively short time, possibly under 300 years, to win these people over and gather them together against Jerusalem; if the Earth had been left completely desolate for 1000 years before they were resurrected, it would take centuries for them to restructure any form of society let alone assemble from the four quarters of the Earth to make war against the beloved city.

The SDA says that this war will not be against Christ and the Saints at the city and temple described by Ezekiel, but instead, it will be against the New Jerusalem that comes down from heaven.[2] Revelation 20 makes it clear that those who come against the camp of the Saints and the beloved city will be devoured by fire coming down from God *before* New Jerusalem descends out of heaven; this makes their claim impossible!

The following chapter of Revelation also informs us that the first heaven and the first Earth had passed away "And there was no more sea" (Revelation 21:1). This tiny detail is incredibly important because it destroys the Adventist claim that Satan and his Army come to battle against the New Jerusalem.

Ezekiel's 38th chapter describes the battle of Gog and Magog as follows:

"'And it shall come to pass at the same time, when Gog shall come against the land of Israel,' says the LORD God, 'that My fury shall come up in My face.

'For in My jealousy, and in the fire of My wrath have I spoken: "Surely in that day, there shall be a great shaking in the land of Israel,

"so that the fishes of the sea, and the fowls of the heaven, and the beasts of the field, and all creeping things that creep upon the earth, and all the men that are upon the face of the earth, shall shake at My presence; and the mountains shall be thrown down, and the steep places shall fall, and every wall shall fall to the ground."'"

(Ezekiel 38:18–20)

If there was "no more sea" just before New Jerusalem descends out of heaven, then how could Satan's army come against it when Ezekiel makes it clear that the fishes and the sea are still very much in existence during the battle of Gog and Magog? This cannot be referring to Armageddon either, as at that time, there was no life in the sea following the second vial judgement. Life will only be restored to the sea by the living waters that proceed out from under the temple where Christ will reign during the millennium of peace. Ezekiel tells how Gog will come against Israel in the latter days, describing God's people as being brought forth out of the nations and dwelling safely without walls, bars or gates. The destruction of Gog will serve as an example to the heathens who witness God's judgement, and the house of Israel will know that He is the LORD, their God.

The closer you look at the SDA claims, the more problems you find. If the dead are raised following the 1000 years in order to be deceived by Satan upon Earth, then this would be the second resurrection; but Scripture tells us that when this army comes against the Holy City, God sends fire down from heaven to devour them. This would mean that they would have suffered a second death, but God makes it clear that the second death only comes *after* judgement and not before it! If all those who are not part of the first resurrection have to go through the great white throne judgement then, according to the Adventists, there would have to be a third resurrection, and a third death for the wicked!

"And as it is appointed unto men once to die, but after this, the judgement." (Hebrews 9:27)

When Revelation spoke of the dead not living again until after the 1000 years were finished, it was part of a condensed list of the end time events. This wasn't speaking of them coming back to life immediately after the millennium, but pointing out that they wouldn't be part of the first resurrection who would live and reign with Christ and be called Blessed and Holy because the second death would have no power over them.

The dead are only raised to face God's judgement for their actions during their life upon Earth, not to get a second chance; this is why the choices we make in this life are so important. The people whom Satan is allowed to deceive following the millennial reign are the descendants of those who survived Armageddon and who replenished the Earth during the 1000-year reign of Christ. When the Earth is fully inhabited, all nations will have full knowledge of Christ and God and, once again, be given the choice between good and evil as God separates the wheat from the tares for the final time and gathers the wheat into the New Jerusalem.

"And I heard a great voice out of heaven saying, 'Behold, the tabernacle of God is with men, and He will dwell with them, and they shall be His people, and God Himself shall be with them and be their God.

'And God shall wipe away all tears from their eyes, and there shall be no more death, neither sorrow, nor crying; neither shall there be any more pain, for the former things are passed away.'"

(Revelation 21:3–4)

1&2   White, Ellen G., *The Great Controversy Between Christ and Satan*, chapter 42: The Controversy Ended. 1888. The International Tract Society Ltd., Watford, Herts, UK.

BIBLIOGRAPHY AND
RECOMMENDED READING

Chiniquy, Charles, *Fifty Years in the Church of Rome*, Fleming H. Revell Co., New York. 1886.

Close, Albert, *"Babylon" The Scarlet Woman or the Divine Foreview of the Church of Rome*, Marshall Brothers Ltd., London and Edinburgh. 1910.

Close, Albert, *The Divine Programme of the World's History*, The Protestant Truth Society, London. 1916.

Cooper, Bill, *The Forging of Codex Sinaiticus*, The Creation Science Movement, Portsmouth, England. 2016.

Dalton, Edward, *The Jesuits: Their Principles and Acts*, W. H. Dalton, London. 1843.

D'Aubigne, Jean-Henri M., *History of the Reformation of the Sixteenth Century*, Oliver and Boyd, Edinburgh. 1847.

Discipulus, *Foretold and Fulfilled: The Church of Rome a Sign of the End*, The Covenant Publishing Co Ltd., London. 1926.

Guinness, Henry G., *The City of the Seven Hills*, James Nisbet and Co, London. 1891.

Guinness, Henry G., *The Divine Programme of the World's History*, Hodder and Stourton, London. 1888.

Guinness, Henry G., *Romanism and the Reformation from the Standpoint of Prophecy*, A. C. Armstrong and Son, New York. 1887.

Hislop, Rev Alexander, *The Two Babylons*, A&C Black Ltd., London. 1939.

Jones, A. H. M., *Constantine and the Conversion of Europe*, Hodder and Stourton Ltd., London. 1948.

Lehmann, L. H., *Out of the Labyrinth*, Agora Publishing Company, New York. 1947.

Manhattan, Avro, *The Catholic Church Against the Twentieth Century*, C. A. Watts & Co Ltd., London. 1949.

McDonald, John, *Romanism Analysed in the Light of Scripture, Reason and History*, Scottish Reformation Society, Edinburgh. 1894.

Muston, Rev D. Alexis, *The Israel of the Alps: A History of the Persecutions of the Waldenses*, Ingram Cook & Co, London. 1853.

Paris, Edmond, *The Secret History of the Jesuits*, Chick Publications, California. 1975.

Paris, Edmond, *The Vatican Against Europe*, P. R. Macmillan Ltd., London. 1961.

Porcelli, Baron, *The Antichrist, His Portrait and History*, Protestant Truth Society, London. 1929.

Ranke, Leopold, *The History of the Popes*, Henry G. Bohn, London. 1848.

Ridley, F. A., *The Jesuits: A Study in Counter Revolution*, Martin Secker and Warburg Ltd., London. 1938.

Saussy, F. T., *Rulers of Evil Useful Knowledge About Governing Bodies*, Osprey Bookmakers, Nevada, U.S.A. 1999.

Smith, Uriah, *Daniel and the Revelation*, The Stanborough Press Ltd., Watford, Herts, UK (SDA Publication). 1921.

Stannus, Hugh. H., *History of the Origin of the Doctrine of the Trinity in the Christian Church*, Christian Life Publishing Company, London. 1883.

Stuart, P. D., *Codeword Barbelon*, Lux, Verbi Books. 2009.

Wainwright, S., *Ritualism, Romanism and the Reformation*, S. W. Partridge & Co, London. 1879.

Walsh, Walter, *England's Fight With the Papacy*, James Nisbet & Co Ltd., London. 1912.

Walsh, Walter, *History of the Romeward Movement in the Church of England 1833-1864*, James Nisbet & Co Ltd., London. 1900.

Walsh, Walter, *The Jesuits in Great Britain*, George Routledge & Sons Ltd., London. 1903.

Walsh, Walter, *The Secret History of the Oxford Movement*, Swan Sonnenschein & Co Ltd., London. 1898.

White, Ellen G., *The Great Controversy Between Christ and Satan During the Christian Dispensation*, The International Tract Society Ltd., Watford, Herts, UK. 1888. (SDA Publication)

White, Percy E., *The Doctrine of the Trinity Analytically Examined and Refuted*, Christadelphian Scripture Study Service, Australia. 1996.

Woodrow, Ralph, *Babylon Mystery Religion*, Ralph Woodrow Evangelistic Association Inc., California. 1981.

Wylie, Rev James A., *The History of Protestantism*, Cassell Petter & Galpin London, Paris & New York. 1899.

Wylie, Rev James A., *The Papacy: It's History, Dogmas, Genius and Prospects*, Hamilton, Adams & Co., London. 1889.

AUTHOR PROFILE

Rob Allcock was born in 1969 in Wolverhampton, England, where he still lives today. He was a competitive rifle shooter and worked for twenty-six years as a Prosthetic Technician until the alleged "Pandemic" of 2020 ended his career.

In 2016, Rob became a Christian after a series of incredible events left him with no choice but to believe in the God of the Bible. *A House Built on Sand* is a compilation of the extensive research he carried out following this revelation, and the enforced lockdowns gave him the opportunity to put pen to paper and share his findings.

Rob is not, and never has been, part of any church or denomination, but believes that a personal relationship with Christ, based on the uncorrupted teachings of Scripture, is more important than fellowship that is not founded on truth.

What Did You Think of *A House Built on Sand*?

A big thank you for purchasing this book. It means a lot that you chose this book specifically from such a wide range on offer. I do hope you enjoyed it.

Book reviews are incredibly important for an author. All feedback helps them improve their writing for future projects and for developing this edition. If you are able to spare a few minutes to post a review on Amazon, that would be much appreciated..

Publisher Information

rowanvale
books

Rowanvale Books provides publishing services to independent authors, writers and poets all over the globe. We deliver a personal, honest and efficient service that allows authors to see their work published, while remaining in control of the process and retaining their creativity. By making publishing services available to authors in a cost-effective and ethical way, we at Rowanvale Books hope to ensure that the local, national and international community benefits from a steady stream of good quality literature.

For more information about us, our authors or our publications, please get in touch.

www.rowanvalebooks.com
info@rowanvalebooks.com

.

www.ingramcontent.com/pod-product-compliance
Lightning Source LLC
Chambersburg PA
CBHW062203080426
42734CB00010B/1776